PHILLIS WHEATLEY
Negro Slave

PHILLIS WHEATLEY

NEGRO SLAVE OF
MR. JOHN WHEATLEY OF BOSTON

by

Marilyn Jensen

Lion Books, Publishers

Dedication

"In loving memory of Mother and Dad . . ."

THIS IS A LION BOOK

Published by LION BOOKS
POB 1337
Scarsdale, N.Y. 10583

ISBN: 0-87460-326-9

Printed in the United States

Acknowledgments:

Every book printed has to be the combined work of many, and this one is no exception. A mere thank you seems so inadequate for such dedicated people as the librarians at the Huntington Library, San Marino, California, the Whittier College Library, Whittier Public Library, and Whittwood Branch Library, Whittier, California, all of whom were so helpful in every phase of my research. A special thanks to the Reverend Hans Holborn of Whittier, California, whose century old material on the History of Methodism shed so much light on the characters of both the Countess of Huntingdon and George Whitefield, and to members of the Writer's Club of Whittier, whose members not only critiqued the manuscript for me but were there with moral support when I needed it. And finally, thanks to my four children who more than once had to take a temporary back seat to "Mom's book," and to my editor, Harriet Ross, who in that first submission saw the promise of what Phillis' story could become and then provided the guidance needed to make it into a far better book. Every one of these people share in the by-line, because I could never have done it alone.

M.J.

CHAPTER I

1761

SUSANNAH WHEATLEY knew she had overslept even before glancing at the clock, for her husband's side of the bed was empty, his nightclothes folded limply over the back of a chair. She was startled to see it was past seven o'clock in the morning. She *never* slept this late; for, in her Puritan conscience she firmly believed no daylight hour should be wasted but filled with meaningful work. And, of all days. The last thing John had said to her last night was that they must get an early start if they were to get to the slave market before the time to open his shop.

Not that she was looking forward to buying a slave. It was one thing to own the three which had belonged to her parents, quite another to go out and buy one like a side of beef. But there was no putting it off this time as she had done before. Sukey, the cook; Dora, the housemaid; and Prince, who did the outside work were no longer young. The time had come to get a strong young girl, twelve or thirteen years old, while the others were still around, able to train her.

She dressed quickly as she organized the day in her mind. She was a small dignified looking woman, angular in both face and body, her blue eyes commanding, as well as promising, honesty and respect. She buttoned her sacque dress, then pulled her gray hair back off her wide brow and anchored it with a bun.

John was just finishing his breakfast as she entered the dining room. How she loved the strength in those broad shoulders, proud of the fact he had not let himself grow paunchy. As always, he wore well cut conservative clothes, his linen stock plain, his colors dark. A smile played around the corners of her mouth. No doubt about it, she had married well.

"There you are," he said as he caught sight of her. "I was about to see what was keeping you. Had you forgotten our plans this morning?"

"I remembered. I just needed a bit more sleep." She picked up a plate from the huge mahogany sideboard. Apparently, the twins, Nathaniel and Mary, had already finished; for the serving dishes were nearly empty. They had grown up so fast. By this time next year, Nat would be in Harvard while Mary could very well be spoken for.

Susannah rather hoped not. Although she certainly would not want spinsterhood for her only daughter, these last few years had been happy ones as Mary increasingly shared the responsibility for managing their home. The arrangement was ideal for both; for, to Susannah, running a household was a duty, something one must do with the same sense of dedication with which a man supported his family. But to Mary it was something more; as though a batch of soap of just the right consistency or a well turned collar represented the ultimate in human achievement.

John pushed back his chair. "I'll have Prince ready the carriage while you eat," he said. "Perhaps, if we find our girl quickly, you can stop by the shop with me. Pick out a length of velvet for yourself and something for Mary. Wait until you see the new shipment from London . . ." His gray eyes sparkled as he mentally caressed the materials he imported and made up into clothing for his customers.

"I'd love that," she said. Bless him for sensing she was not overjoyed at the prospect of visiting the noisy smelly slave market, knowing full well she would rather select fabrics than slaves.

Once in the carriage she impulsively slipped her hand in his, feeling an answering squeeze as Prince guided them through the narrow cobbled streets. She loved the peculiar conglomeration of sights, sounds, and smells that were Boston; the mingled scents of fish, tar, and spices wafting up from Long Wharf at the end of their street, where ships tied up between voyages to and from the West Indies, the Orient, and England, their hulls rising and falling with the tides; town criers calling out news of newly arrived ships, town meetings, and weddings; chimney sweeps darting in and out of alleys like flies. And the bells. They tolled for the dead, opened up markets, summoned one to church. Susannah knew each by its tone, one sombre, another melodious, others badly off-tone. She loved it all from the north end, where she had grown up alongside the Hutchinsons and the Reveres, to the narrow neck connecting the town to the mainland, guarded by the high brick arch which bade farewell or welcomed, depending upon which direction one was headed.

"Let us out here," John directed Prince as they approached the slave market across from the Boston Common, "then go by my shop. Tell them I've been detained, and come back and wait for us."

"Yessir." Prince's leathery black face was impassive as he started the horses moving.

At the slave market, Susannah winced as she watched a huge bearded man, whip in hand, herd a group of slaves onto a weatherbeaten platform, lashing out at a woman who stumbled on the rickety steps. The whip missed its target, but they heard it snap, saw the slaves cringe in terror along the platform edge.

Accustomed to thinking of slavery in terms of well-cared-for servants like their own, Susannah was horrified to see that half of this group were children. "I've never seen anything so disgraceful," she cried, her usually gentle voice sharp with indignation. "None of these poor creatures are properly clothed, and they all look half-starved."

"I know." John's voice was grim. "The whole business is deplorable. Unfortunately, it can't be helped. There is nothing we can do except work toward changing the laws so slavery can be abolished. Meanwhile . . ."

Susannah clutched his arm. "That child . . . He's going to strike her . . . Somebody stop him."

The child looked no more than six or seven years old, so emaciated she appeared to be all bones.

"Move, I tell you," the man bellowed. Over there . . ." He yanked her by the arm and shoved her to the edge of the platform.

"Good Lord," Susannah breathed. She shuddered as she edged her way to the platform with John close behind. The child's eyes were wide with terror. A ragged piece of carpet covered her from just under the armpits to the knees, frayed strings hanging down where it had unraveled.

"He could have killed her." Emotion blurred Susannah's voice, almost uncontrollable now.

"He doesn't dare," John replied, but she knew by the way his cheek muscle quivered he was as angry as she.

"Can't we do something?" she cried out. She had never felt so helpless.

"I wish we could, but what?" He sighed. "These things have existed for a long time, my dear. They are acting within the limits of the law."

"Then the laws must be changed. I just never realized how degrading it is. I'd like to banish everyone connected with it, beginning with that man right there." She felt her face hot with anger, not caring who heard her.

Heads nodded in sympathy; others had amused looks. She knew she shouldn't be making a public spectacle of herself, but this was not the first time she had embarrassed John with her outspoken views.

The auctioneer stepped to the edge of the platform. "Just brought this cargo from the west end of Africa. One hundred fifty of 'em. Every one strong and healthy." He spat onto the ground below. "See? They all got pockmarks so's you don't have to worry."

He looked down at the Wheatleys, and his thick lips parted in a grin. "How about a wench to lighten the lady's load?"

Susannah turned away. She couldn't bear to look at him. The child's eyes reminded her of an animal she had once seen caught in a trap many years ago. The comparison catapulted her into action. "You must buy her," she said abruptly to John.

His eyebrows shot up. "Don't let your heart rule your head, my dear. We're looking for someone to be of some help to you. A strong wind would snap this one right in two."

"John Wheatley, will you stop talking like you're buying a piece of furniture? She's a live human being." She breathed deeply, then with restrained firmness said, "You must buy her. It's our Christian duty to see she has a good home. I shall never be able to sleep unless we do."

"Susannah, be practical . . ."

"Will your conscience let you leave her here to God only knows what fate?" Her palms grew moist, her heart pounding rapidly as she looked up into his eyes. She *had* to have this child. "Please, John!"

She scarcely breathed as he looked critically at the child then turned to her. "All right."

Relief flooded her senses as she watched John exchange words with the auctioneer. The bidding was to start shortly, he said when he rejoined her, adding he had prevailed on the man to offer the child first so they needn't remain any longer than necessary.

"Perhaps you should go on home with Prince," he suggested. "I can take care of the sale myself."

She shook her head. "No. I will stay." No matter how distasteful it was, she was going to make sure nothing went wrong. She had the distinct feeling she was being guided by a power outside herself, entrusted to oversee the entire matter to its conclusion.

A murmur rippled through the crowd as the auctioneer grabbed the child and jerked her to the front of the platform. "Step up, folks," he began. "Here's a useful wench. Small, but wiry. Speak up. What am I offered?"

John's opening bid was immediately topped by another.

"Bid again." Susannah whispered, clenching her hands so tight the fingernails cut into her palms.

John upped the bid.

Susannah was sure it was an act of providence when the child was suddenly seized with a violent spasm of coughing and the bidding stopped at once. The child, along with a bill of sale, was handed over to John. Within minutes, they were back in the carriage headed towards home.

The sharp sea air was strong in their nostrils as they passed the State House and turned onto King Street. Between them the child sat rigid, staring straight ahead. She had not appeared to move a muscle since leaving the marketplace.

What was locked up in her mind? What must she have endured? Weeks, months of cruelty on the slaveship. Susannah was sure of that. Were her parents dead or alive? Had they been sold into slavery too? *Oh, child, if you could only talk.*

The child stared straight ahead, unblinking.

CHAPTER II

SUSANNAH felt the pride she always did as they stopped midblock in front of their home. It was a pretty house, with its freshly painted white trim that Prince washed down every day to keep spotless, and smoke curling out of the chimney in long lazy spirals.

From the front it was impossible to see the one story wooden ell, the original house to which John had brought her as a bride. It was after his business began to prosper they had added the second story in front, making it one of the handsomest homes on King Street.

Susannah was touched to see how gently Prince lowered the child down from the carriage and how careful he was to keep her covered.

John remained in the carriage, for he had to go on to the shop. So much for the plans to look at the new fabrics. No matter. Right now there were more important matters to attend to. Susannah took the child's bony hand in hers and together they went inside. "Sukey," she called.

The old cook wiped her gnarled hands on a corner of her white apron and lumbered into the hallway. "Yes, M'am,

we're about done makin' the soap," she began. Catching sight
of the child her jaw dropped, her eyes widened into huge
white circles. "Land sakes, you must've bought the puniest
one there. Dora," she called, "come see what we got here."

The younger woman, duster in hand, gaped at the child
then wrinkled her nose. "She stinks."

She was right. The odor overpowered them now that they
were inside. "Sukey, go find Miss Mary," Susannah directed.
"She can help us clean her up."

"Yes'm." Sukey retreated down the hallway muttering to
herself.

Susannah turned to Dora. "Bring hot water and lots of soap
and towels out to the bathhouse."

"Yes, M'am." Dora looked at the child and grinned. "Good
thing we made lots of soap this morning. We sure goin' to
need it."

In the bathhouse, the child pressed close to Susannah as
Sukey and Dora bustled in and out carrying jugs of steaming
water, laying out towels. Mary appeared in the doorway; a
younger version of her mother, her fair hair curled around
her white dust cap, a simple flowered dress flattering her
slim figure.

"So you really did go to the auction." Her eyes widened at
the sight of the image before her. "Such a scrawny little
thing."

"Never mind, get to work," said Susannah briskly. "Dora,
run across to the Seymors and see if you can borrow some
clothes. Their Bessie is about the same size. Tell them you
need everything from skin out."

Mary knelt down and took the child's small hand in hers.
"You poor little thing," she said softly. Slowly, like a new-
born baby's, the small fingers curled around the larger ones.
"Shouldn't we get her something to eat?" Mary asked her
mother.

"First things first," Susannah answered. "We'll get her

clean and then worry about food. Here, help me get her into the tub."

The child fought savagely as they lowered her into the water, but once in, the warmth seemed to soothe her. Quieted down, she scrunched up at one end and watched them warily.

"Now how we gonna get you clean if you stays up there, child?" Sukey demanded. "Come on down here."

But the child did not budge.

"You gonna scrub the skin right off her?" Dora protested to Sukey as she maneuvered the child into a position where she could get at her. Sukey began scrubbing vigorously.

Mary gasped. "I've never seen so much dirt."

"That's 'cause you never seen the ships they came across on." Dora's voice was bitter. Her dark eyes flashed.

Susannah sighed. Although Dora had never known real hardship, she was full of tales gleaned from other slaves about the rat-infested holds of the human cargo ships, the filthy customs houses where slaves were crowded in so tight they couldn't move, many of them dying before they could be brought to the market place.

Sukey had the child out of the tub now, rubbing the caramel brown skin until it glowed. She was like a kitten, wild one minute, docile the next. With Mary holding her, they managed to slip the borrowed brown calico dress over the petticoat, and over that a matching bodice. Sukey gathered up the excess evenly on all sides and laced up the front. "There, how's that?" she asked the others as she began the tedious task of brushing the matted hair and braiding it in tiny plaits all over the child's head. Sukey sighed. "How this child came clear cross on that ship without getting lice, I'll never know."

"Now," said Susannah, "what shall we feed her?"

"I got just the thing," Sukey replied.

Back in the kitchen she lifted the lid off the pot where crusts cut off from yesterday's bread simmered in milk. Susannah nodded approval. Nothing fancy. Just good and nourishing. Although John made a good living, there had been too many lean years for her to tolerate waste.

Sukey ladled some into a bowl and set it on the table.

"Come, dear," Susannah said.

But the child stiffened, grabbing Susannah's skirt with her small fist. Gently, with Mary's help, they managed to seat her at the table, but getting food into her proved impossible. The harder they tried to get her to open her mouth, the tighter her jaw clamped shut.

Sukey folded her arms over her massive bosom. "Don't you worry. I've seen 'em before when they first comes across. This child is just like a baby. She got to learn our ways. Don't you worry none. Sukey'll teach her all she needs to know."

Susannah was grateful Sukey seemed equal to the challenge. She already foresaw problems she had not anticipated.

The child remained close to Sukey. Susannah was struck by the delicate beauty she had fleetingly noticed at the dock. Barely glimpsed earlier, she now saw it in vivid detail. The thick black hair, the well shaped head, the high sensitive brow. She glanced at the slim hands with long delicate fingers tapering to a point. Those hands were not meant for hard work. She would have to train her as a personal maid, teach her to care for her wardrobe, style her hair, tasks requiring a gentle touch.

"What you gonna call her?" Sukey's question broke into Susannah's thoughts.

Susannah had already given it some consideration. "I had a friend long ago. Her name was Phillis." She paused. "I always thought it a beautiful name. I wanted to name you that, Mary, but your father preferred family names."

"I never heard you mention this Phillis," Mary said.

"She died when I was twelve, but I've never forgotten her." She mused, "I wonder if she would mind my naming a servant after her."

"I don't think so," Mary said.

"Mighty fancy name for a child what's gonna work in the kitchen," Sukey said.

But Susannah's mind was made up. "Phillis it shall be. Sukey, you keep her with you while we fix up a place for her to sleep."

Sukey began crooning softly as they left the room. The child stared at her, head cocked to one side.

CHAPTER III

THEY HAD PLANNED to put Phillis out back with the others.

"But it's so drafty out there, and with that cough that she has ... Besides, suppose she wakes up at night? She'd be frightened out of her wits," Mary protested.

"She won't be alone," Susannah pointed out. "Dora and Sukey will be right there."

"A lot of good that will do. Dora would be no help; and Sukey's getting so deaf she'd never hear her," Mary countered. "Let her sleep with me for now. Just until she gets used to us."

"I suppose it's all right if your father agrees. I certainly don't know where else to put her."

To Mary's surprise, he merely nodded and said, "Might as well protect our investment. No sense her getting sick before she's any use to us."

Sleeping arrangements out of the way, they tackled the problem of getting Phillis to eat. It was Sukey who came up with the idea of putting her food into gourds. "It's probably what she's used to," she explained. "Looks to me like we gotta get her used to our ways a little at a time."

Phillis sniffed the contents suspiciously when the gourd

was offered, then, apparently satisfied, took a tentative sip. At the first taste her eyes brightened as she grabbed the vessel in both hands and emptied it in big noisy gulps.

"Land sakes, child," exclaimed Sukey. "You licked it so clean it almost looks like I washed it myself."

From then on, it became a real challenge to keep the child filled up. She was forever grabbing a handful of something out of the pantry and stuffing it into her mouth, leaving a trail of crumbs behind.

"No wonder she's hungry," Dora told them. "You know what they feed 'em on slave ships? Just yams 'n rice 'n sometimes horse beans, that's all. And not enough of them to keep 'em more than half alive."

It was not long before they all admitted the child had made quite an impact on them. Even Nat. He had frightened her the first day as he bounded into the kitchen, threw his books on the floor, and thundered, "What's there to eat?"; but Sukey had bent down to Phillis and whispered, "This here is Mr. Nat. He won't hurt you. And, honey, you better like him 'cause he's my favorite person in this whole house."

Somehow reassured by Sukey's confidential tone, Phillis had visibly relaxed, and within a few days followed Nat everywhere, listening each afternoon when it was time for him to come home from school.

The one thing nobody could get her to do was talk.

"There's something wrong with her," Dora said.

But Mary disagreed. She could not shake the feeling that this child was bright, although the others were skeptical when she mentioned it to them.

"I don't care what you think," she said during supper at the end of Phillis' first week with them. "I'm going to teach her more than just household chores. I may even teach her to read and write."

Her father looked unimpressed. "Remember, we bought her to help your mother."

"I know, but think how nice it will be if Phillis can read to her."

Nat came close to choking on his food. "You're daft."

"Few slaves are capable of such accomplishments, Mary," Susannah said. "However, I suppose there is no harm in your trying. It will give you something to do over the summer. But don't expect too much."

Before going to bed that night, Mary dug out the old Hornbook she had used many years ago in Dame Cooper's school. She would prove that they were wrong about Phillis. She knew it as well as she knew her own name.

Such a strange little creature, she thought, looking at the sleeping figure underneath the bright puff quilt. For days, she had awakened before everyone and slipped off somewhere all by herself. One morning she had been asleep when Mary called her; but when she crawled out of bed, the small forehead was smudged with dirt, and her nightgown was damp around the bottom.

Then one day Mary had awakened to find Phillis' bed empty. Hurrying downstairs she had reached the kitchen just in time to hear the sound of glass splintering on the back steps. Outside she found Phillis shaking with fright as she stared at the shattered remains of a water pitcher.

"The poor little thing acted like she thought I was going to beat her," Mary told her mother later. "I tried to make her understand it was all right, but she wouldn't touch her breakfast."

Tomorrow, Mary vowed as she made ready for bed, she would wake early enough to see just what these early morning pilgrimages were all about.

It was not yet light when she awoke, but Phillis was already stirring in the next bed. Mary closed her eyes until she heard her tiptoe out of the room and down the stairs. Sliding out of bed, she slipped a banyon over her nightdress and followed, surprised to see her mother at the head of the stairs.

"I heard her go past my door," Susannah said. "Let's see where she goes."

Downstairs, they found the back door open; and out of the corner of her eye Mary noted the water pitcher was missing from the kitchen table.

Outside, they followed the narrow path past the smoke house, slowing their steps as they reached the House of Necessity. Ahead of them Phillis stood beside the well, her back to them. Silhouetted on the rock ledge at the top of the well was the water pitcher.

Fascinated, they watched her draw up a bucketful of water and pour it into the pitcher, then, pitcher in hand, turn toward the east where slivers of pale pink were beginning to streak the sky.

"What's she doing?" Mary whispered.

Susannah cautioned silence. "Sssh, whatever this is, we mustn't spoil it for her."

At the precise moment the sun broke through the clouds, Phillis raised the pitcher high over her head and poured water onto the ground in a steady stream. Then, pitcher empty, she knelt, placed her forehead in the damp grass, and began crooning in a singsong voice. After a few moments she rose and walked to the house, her small head majestically erect.

Although mystified, they accepted her daily morning ritual, making sure there was always a water pitcher available. It was Sukey who came up with what seemed a plausible explanation.

"She's a Kaffir. Her people are sun worshippers. They always welcome the day like that. Old Moses down the street told me all about it. He says all the ones they bring from the west side of Africa do it."

As the weeks slipped by, Phillis' pre-dawn walks grew less frequent. More often she slept until awakened by the others. By the end of the summer, she had charmed the entire household. Even her master. Until now, John Wheatley had maintained that all slaves should be well treated, but not allowed to mingle freely with the family. Not that he had done anything to dispel such policy, but they all noticed how Phillis ran to the door to greet him when she heard his 'carriage And they noticed, too, how he had taken to having some kind of sweet in his pocket to be dispensed along with a pat on the head.

"She'll be spoiled rotten if he keeps that up," Mary complained. She was beginning to wonder how much longer Phillis was to be allowed the run of the house.

The child now bore little resemblance to the half-starved waif they had first brought home. Her cheeks were filled out, her eyes had lost their haunted look, and her movements were quick and graceful. But she still refused to talk.

"I can't understand it," Mary said to her mother one morning. "I know she understands everything we say. Watch. Where are the apples, Phillis?"

The child's eyes immediately went to the bowl of apples on the sideboard.

"See?" Mary said, exasperated. "I know she could talk if she wanted to."

"The mark of a good teacher is patience," Susannah said. "Didn't I warn you that it wouldn't be easy?"

Mary worked longer than usual with Phillis that day. "Say pitcher." She pointed to the pitcher on the table in front of them; but there was no response. Mary sighed. Were the others right? Would Phillis ever learn? She supposed she should just turn her over to Sukey and forget about lessons; but after the way she had bragged, she knew Nat would never let her forget it if she failed.

"Come on, Phillis," she coaxed. "Say pit-cher." She exaggerated each syllable.

There was a long silence, then "Pit . ." a pucker appeared between Phillis' eyes as she struggled with the sound, "cher," she finished, her eyes bright with triumph.

"Phillis, you did it." Mary jumped up and hugged her. "Mother, Sukey, Phillis can talk."

"Pitcher, pitcher," Phillis babbled as the others came running.

Sukey grinned. "I got a feeling we're just beginning to hear from this child."

She was right. Within weeks, Phillis prattled so incessantly, they almost wished she had never learned to talk.

Spurred by her first success, Mary's plans for Phillis' education rapidly expanded. "I'll have her reading in no time," she boasted; but her enthusiasm was dampened when her father said, "I wonder if you are not spending too much time teaching Phillis things for which she has little use. Remember, the idea in bringing her here was to minister to your mother. After all, I'm a business man. I'll not feed and clothe a growing girl without some return for it."

"But she's learning so much."

"Has she learned to clean a house properly? Prepare a meal? From what others tell me, she has learned little except to talk."

His tone of voice made Mary feel like a little girl again.

"Beginning tomorrow, I shall expect you to spend more time instructing her in household chores. Do you understand?"

"Yes, Father."

His expression softened. "Then, if there is time, and you want to teach her letters or some other foolishness, it is up to you. But she must earn her keep."

The next morning, Mary dutifully began supervising Phillis in household duties, deferring lessons until well after the midday meal . . . But so far as housework was concerned, Phillis left much to be desired. Although eager to learn, her coordination was poor.

"That child's going to break every dish in this house," Dora raved, her face a thundercloud as she swept up the broken fragments of the latest mishap. "Look at that rug where she spilled whale oil. I scrubbed and scrubbed, but it's never going to look the same."

Mary sighed, and admitted Phillis did seem to be making more work instead of less. By common consent, she was relegated to duties like polishing silver, putting away clothes, and winding yarn.

"And when she dusts, make sure there's nothin' she can break on the tables," Sukey warned.

Mary was miffed. "We're none of us good at everything. She's already learning the alphabet."

"Hmmph. Learning letters never did a black child any good," was the old woman's retort.

CHAPTER IV

1762

By Fall of the following year, the family could scarcely recall life without Phillis, a time of happy memories blending together like links in a chain.

She was growing, as Prince put it, "faster than the weeds in the flower beds"; while Susannah complained she outgrew clothes as quickly as they could be made for her. As for her earlier years, Phillis could recall nothing. It was as though she had always lived on King Street.

The air was chilly with frost one day late in October. She hurried, for Nat would be home from Harvard today. If she could finish her chores early, there would be time to read for him. She glanced at the books piled on her desk. He was going to be surprised at her progress since the last time he was home.

She slipped her black workday dress over her head, and nimbly fastened the row of buttons that paraded down the front of the bodice, tied a clean white apron around her waist, then sat on the floor to wrestle with the hated footgear.

Finally she stood up and began brushing her hair. If only it were smooth and golden like Miss Mary's, then brushing might do some good. But even though it was cut close to her head, hers stuck out every which way. She sighed, and gathered the kinky mass up under her dust cap, then turned to the task of straightening her room.

Her room. How she loved the sound of those words. She had known from the first that sharing Mary's room had been a temporary arrangement. She had expected to be moved out with Dora and Sukey; but Susannah had objected. "Too drafty. The way she takes cold, she'll have to sleep in the house." The matter was settled.

Now, months later, Phillis was as thrilled as the day she had moved into the cozy room with its high beamed ceiling, braided rug, canopied bed; the crisp blue and white curtains fluttering in the dormer windows, the mahogany highboy chest polished to a soft reddish glow.

On it she kept her very own bible, presented the day she was baptized, and a single silver candlestick. Next to the fireplace, a washstand held her toilet articles, and a dainty flowered pitcher and basin; and beside the bed, since the day Mary had come upon her scrawling on a brick with a piece of charcoal, a small writing table which had once belonged to Grandmother Wheeler.

She dusted it lovingly, rearranging the books and inkwell from which a quill stood out at a rakish angle, took a last look around, then skipped downstairs to begin her day.

Sukey and Dora were already in the kitchen. Dora scowled, her lips pursed. "About time you got yourself in here, Missy."

Phillis busied herself taking dishes down from the cupboard. "I'm sorry I'm late."

"If you didn't spend all your time reading, you just might be some use around here."

"Leave her be." Sukey said.

But Dora was not to be put off. "All those lessons just makes you think you're too good to work like the rest of us."

Sukey frequently took Phillis' side when Dora picked on her, but this time she merely said, "She's right, child. The sooner you learn us black people weren't meant for book learning, the better off you're gonna be. The good Lord, He put us here to serve white folks and there's no use fightin' it."

Dora's eyes snapped. "The Lord meant for everyone to be free." She uttered an oath as she burned her finger lifting a pot of porridge off the fire.

"Free?" Sukey's frame shook like a bowl of custard before it was set. "Honey, you is dreaming. Black people ain't never gonna be free. Come on now, get that water to boiling. I hear 'em stirring upstairs. Phillis, fill up that jar with molasses. Move!"

Phillis sighed. It wasn't the first time she'd heard them argue, and she wondered who was right.

As soon as her chores were finished, she went to the library to wait for Nat. She loved the big comfortable chairs, the shelves of books covering the walls clear to the ceiling. She ran a finger over the smooth binding. *The Practice of Piety* by Lewis Bayley, Reverend Wigglesworth's *Day of Doom*, several by Cotton Mather, who with his father, Increase Mather, had helped shape the New England conscience. "Someday, I shall read every book in this room," she said aloud.

"You've set yourself quite a task."

She turned to see Nat and Mary in the doorway.

Nat settled himself in the biggest chair, stretching his legs out to their full length. "Mary tells me you're going to read for me."

Mary picked up the Bible from its stand and handed it to Phillis. "I've been telling him how well you are doing. Let's show him."

Phillis opened it to the book of Isaiah and began to read, "Yet now, O Jacob, my servant, and Israel whom I have chosen . . ."

Nat looked astonished. "Mary said you read as well as any grown person, but I thought she was joshing. What do you enjoy reading most?"

"Poetry."

"Indeed. And whose poetry have you read?"

"Miss Mary gave me a copy of Gray's Elegy in a Country Churchyard."

He looked skeptical.

Mary shrugged. "She reads everything she can get her hands on."

"Congratulations," he said. "You must be a first rate teacher."

"It's all her doing."

"Still, a pupil is only as good as her teacher," he answered. "What are you studying now, Phillis?"

"I'm learning how the colonies are governed."

He looked thoughtful. "I believe you could learn anything. Even Latin. Would you like to try?"

"Me learn Latin?" Phillis blinked in astonishment. "I couldn't, Mr. Nat. That's just for gentlemen. Master John said so himself."

Mary looked surprised too. Although she had received a good education at Dame Cooper's, her curriculum had not included Latin. Young ladies, if they went beyond needlework and deportment, were taught history, music, and French, but *never* Latin.

Nat laughed. "Why not? I'll teach you myself."

Phillis watched wide-eyed as he selected a book. Moments later she was repeating after him, "Amo, I love; Amas, you love . . ."

In the months that followed, Phillis continued to grow and learn. Each day it became more apparent she was no ordinary child.

"I've never seen a child grasp things so quickly," Master John said to Susannah.

Susannah confessed that all that was taking place in her home merely strengthened her conviction that the Lord had sent Phillis to them for some special purpose. She did not share how well she understood Phillis' eagerness to grasp facts, and how well she remembered her frustration when Mary had not taken well to learning. She had so wanted a daughter who did more than sew a neat hem.

Phillis, too, began to realize that she was different from the other slaves. It confused her. Even church presented problems. She loved attending services at King's Chapel with the family; although she admitted to Dora she was more impressed by the red velvet vestments and solid silver communion plates, than by the two-hour sermons followed by another hour of prayer for which they had to kneel on the hard wooden boards. Only fear of being tickled on the ear by the tithing man kept her awake; for she knew what that fur-tipped rod was for. Worse yet was the fear she might be ridiculed from the pulpit. She had seen it happen to others who snored instead of listening. Whenever she felt her head begin to nod, she pinched herself to stay awake while the minister droned on and on.

The first Sunday she had attended with the family, she had no idea her mistress was breaking a long standing tradition by having her sit with the family, rather than in the upstairs gallery with the other slaves. She found out much later when Sukey told her, it was undoubtedly the reason for the coolness she had encountered among the congregation. Susannah had squelched it at once, introducing Phillis to church members in a way which made it impossible for them not to respond; and aside from a few raised eyebrows, nothing was said. But Phillis becoming sensitive, had felt the antagonism, had seen the cold eyes appraising her.

"Anyone else would never got permission for you to sit downstairs," Sukey told her. "They don't dare refuse Miss Susannah anything; 'cause Master John's the one gave so much money when they built the new church. They got to let you sit anywhere she wants, 'cause they're afraid he'll up and join another church."

Phillis tried not to let it bother her. She had heard the pastor say, "love thy neighbor"; but she sensed there were a lot of people who didn't love her.

And at home, Miss Susannah permitted Phillis little time to spend with Sukey, Prince, and Dora; expecting her to instead spend evenings in the parlor with the family. Phillis said nothing; but she missed the time when she used to gather with the others in servant's quarters and sing. And she missed Dora's gossip. More and more, it seemed Miss Susannah was trying to pretend Phillis wasn't a servant at all.

It bothered her, especially the week she was confined to the house because of the weather. Sheets of water bathed the windowpanes. It was the third straight day of rain. One more needlework stitch, or one more skein of linen, and she knew she would lose her mind. By midafternoon the rain had stopped; but she knew her mistress would say it was too wet to go outside.

"Prince is 'bout to go to the market," Sukey told her. "He said if you want to go with him, you can."

Susannah hesitated when Phillis asked permission. "I don't know if it would be wise. You're coughing again; and the air is so damp."

"Please, Miss Susannah? I'll bundle up warm."

Susannah's nod was reluctant. "Be sure you use the foot warmer."

"I will. Thank you."

They stayed at the market longer than they had intended. A stiff wind was blowing by the time they started home.

"Let me ride up front with you so I can see better," Phillis said as Prince helped her into the carriage.

He scratched his head. "I don't know, Phillis. Miss Susannah said be sure and keep you warm. It's mighty cold up here."

She stomped her foot. "I won't catch cold. Please, Prince. I don't want to sit back there by myself." At his assenting nod, she hopped up on the seat before he could change his mind.

Susannah had obviously been waiting for their return. She rushed out to meet the carriage as Prince pulled up in front of the house. Phillis sensed immediately that something was wrong. Except for two flaming spots high on her cheekbones, her mistress' face was milk white, her eyes dark with anger, her mouth compressed in a thin straight line. Prince looked scared. Phillis shivered.

"Do but look at the saucy varlet," Mrs. Wheatley exclaimed. "If he hasn't the impudence to sit upon the same seat as *my* Phillis? I'll not have it."

"But it wasn't his fault. I made him let me," Phillis cried.

"Take care of the carriage," Susannah snapped, "and see it doesn't happen again, or I shall be obliged to speak to Mr. Wheatley about it."

"Yess'm." Prince's shoulders drooped, and the corners of his mouth turned down.

Prince humiliated, was dismissed. She put her arm around Phillis. "Come, dear. We'll have Dora bring hot water so you can soak your feet; You must be frozen."

At suppertime, Phillis tried to eat; but it was no use. As soon as she could, she took Prince a plate of johnnycake just off the fire. "I'm sorry," she said. "I tried to explain, but she wouldn't listen."

"That's all right." Prince's voice was gentle, but the hurt showed in his eyes. Phillis was unable to shake the feeling something had gone from their relationship, that it would never be quite the same again.

"Sukey, am I different?" Phillis asked the day after the incident with Prince, as she pressed freshly churned butter into molds.

Sukey stirred a bubbling kettle of soup, took a sip, scowled, and reached for the salt. "What you mean, *different?*" She emphasized the first syllable of the word.

"I'm not sure. It's—well—I'm not like you or Dora, but I can't be like Miss Mary either, so who am I?"

Sukey put a lid on the pot. There was compassion in her dark eyes as she said, "Child, you can't help being what the good Lord made you. You've got a grown up mind in a little girl body; and the trouble is you don't really fit nowhere. You sound more like white folk than black; and you're smarter then most of 'em, but most white folk don't want black folk sitting at their tables, so you just never gonna be the right color." She wiped her hands on her apron. "It ain't gonna be easy, nosiree." She shook her head then reached for a silver tray and handed it to Phillis. "Now don't you go bothering your head about it anymore. There ain't nothing you can do about it anyway. Here, fix up this tray. Miss Susannah's got company up in her sitting room. Make it fancy now. It's her cousin and that neighbor of hers."

Phillis enjoyed arranging the rich cakes, the delicate candied fruits, the heavy silver pot with steaming, fragrant tea.

The ladies were seated on the settee as Phillis set the tray on the low table in front of them. She recognized Susannah's cousin, Martha Bates, and a friend, Abigail Ridgeway. Both ladies were gowned in opulent silk, their hair done in elaborate styles.

"Thank you, Phillis. Sit down and join us," Susannah said as she prepared to pour.

Phillis glanced at the guests, then at the tea tray. "I'm afraid I forgot the sugar. I'd best go get it."

As she retreated through the doorway, she had seen the visitors draw themselves up in rigid disapproval at Susannah's invitation for her to stay. Upon returning with the sugar she heard Mrs. Bates say, "Susannah, I can't believe it's you behaving this way. Frankly, I have been meaning to speak to you about it. I'm afraid, my dear, you are becoming the talk of Boston." Her voice softened. "I know you've always wanted more children, but a negro slave child? *Really*."

Her voice trailed off, but Phillis could picture the raised eyebrow, the slightly flared nostril accompanying the haughty tone. She remained where she was, knowing she could not return to the room.

"Martha, and you too, Abigail," Susannah's tone was icy, its fury unmistakable. "This is my home. How I conduct myself with my servants is none of your concern. I have asked Phillis to join us; and if you do not wish to sit at the same table you are free to leave."

There was an audible gasp, then silence. Still clutching the sugar bowl, Phillis quietly descended the stairs to the kitchen, her stomach contorted into a painful knot. She couldn't bear being the cause of alienating her mistress from anyone. Maybe Sukey was right. God created people different colors; and maybe He didn't mean for them to sit at the same table.

"What's the trouble, child?" Sukey asked when Phillis appeared.

"I—I don't feel well. May I go to my room?"

Sukey looked concerned. "You comin' down with another of them colds?"

Phillis shook her head. "No." She thrust the sugar bowl

into Sukey's hand. "Please take this upstairs."

Sukey nodded. "You go on. I'll fetch it up. But child, you don't fool me. Something happened up there, didn't it?"

There was no answer as Phillis fled to her room.

CHAPTER V

1765

WHILE PHILLIS grappled with identity problems a series of events had begun which would drastically affect not only her life but that of every colonist.

When news reached Boston in 1763 that a treaty had been signed marking the official end of the French and Indian War, it is doubtful anyone realized it was the first step toward American independence, but within two years a few far-sighted individuals such as Paul Revere, Samuel Adams, and John Hancock were beginning to realize the fuse had been lit. The new Stamp Act was the catalyst, Parliament's method of forcing the colonies to pay their share of the long costly war. It required that as of November 1, 1765 broadsides, legal documents, and all other forms of printed communication must bear a government stamp.

On the surface life went on as usual, but people seethed at being taxed by a government in which they had no voice.

The Sons of Liberty soon became a household word. "Rabble rousers," they were dubbed by the more conservative citizens, among them John Wheatley.

But far more upsetting to the Wheatleys than politics was Nat's announcement he was leaving school to learn the merchant business.

"Master John's in a temper about Mr. Nat quitting Harvard," Sukey said as she and Phillis sat in the kitchen shelling peas. "Miss Susannah looks like she's been crying all night."

They looked up as Mary appeared in the doorway.

"Sukey, Mother asked if you've baked anything to serve when the Reverend Mr. Occom comes to tea tomorrow."

"You can tell her I made one of my sugar cakes," Sukey answered, then muttered, "though why I got to make somethin' fancy to serve an Indian I'll never know."

"An Indian? A real live one?" Phillis asked.

Mary laughed. "A real live one. Mr. Occom's a minister, and he's here in Boston to raise money to build a school for Indian children."

"Why is he coming to our house?"

"Mother met him when he preached at our church last year. Now she wants to help him."

Sukey grinned. "If Miss Susannah was a man she'd go right out and raise the money herself."

Phillis was amazed in mid-afternoon when Susannah excused her from her duties. "Go upstairs and change your dress, dear, then join us in the library. Mr. Occom has sent word he especially wants to meet you."

Why, Phillis wondered, as she donned her heavy black Sunday dress, took special care to see that her white cap sat straight on her curls. She skipped downstairs two at a time, slowing to a more sedate pace just before reaching the library.

"Come in," Susannah directed as Phillis hesitated at the door. "Mr. Occom, I should like you to meet our Phillis."

The man's piercing black eyes lighted up as he stepped

forward and smiled. "So this is the little girl I've heard so much about. How old are you, child?"

"Twelve, sir."

His skin was a dark reddish brown, unlike any she had ever seen, and the straight heavy brows told her the hair under the powdered wig must be as black as hers. He was dressed like any other gentleman, far different from the tales she had heard of half-naked savages who scalped helpless women and children.

"I'm happy to meet you, Phillis. Your mistress tells me you are pursuing your subjects diligently."

"Yes, sir."

"Good. I hope you will keep me informed of her progress," he said to Susannah, then turned back to Phillis. "Might I ask which among these books are your favorites?" He gestured toward the shelves behind them.

Without a moment's hesitation she answered, "The Bible, Collected Tales of Mythology, and Pope's Homer."

"Admirable taste, my dear, especially the first one. You can never study the Bible too much."

Phillis liked him. He was Mohegan, he told her, converted to Christianity at the age of seventeen by a missionary who came to their village.

"I decided I'd learn to read so I could study the Bible myself instead of waiting for someone to read it to me." After that, he told them, he went to Dr. Wheelock's school in a nearby village, the same school which was now too small to do the job of educating all the Indians who came asking to be admitted. "And so I am on my way to London to raise money for a bigger school." He turned to Phillis. "Always remember, child, live by God's word and learn all you can. Then use that knowledge to make this a better world for others."

"He was so nice," Phillis said later to Mary. "I think I'll write to him while he's in England."

"I think he'd like that," Mary said. "I'm sure he'll be lonely so far away from his family. Mother says he may be there two years or more."

Phillis posted her first letter to him soon afterward and some months later received one in reply telling of his safe arrival and his meeting with the Earl of Dartmouth, whom the King had appointed chairman of the committee to raise funds for the school.

"How lucky he is to be able to go to London," Phillis said wistfully when she showed the letter to Susannah.

The Reverend Mr. Occom's admonition for Phillis to learn all she could seemed easy enough to follow, but something was wrong. What had once delighted the family as she explored new vistas and increasingly expressed her thoughts in letters and compositions was causing problems.

What had gone wrong, Susannah wondered as she and John made ready for bed one evening some months after Occom's visit. It seemed as though everyone in the house had some kind of complaint, and they all concerned Phillis.

"I declare, if that child don't quit sneakin' off with a book in the middle of what's to be done around here," Sukey had raged just this morning.

And now here was Master John angry because he had discovered Phillis leaving every lamp in the house unlit to go off in a corner to write poetry.

"Poetry?" Susannah couldn't help feeling a touch of pride. "Are you sure?" she asked.

"Here it is." He drew a scrap of paper out of his pocket and handed it to her.

With a growing sense of wonder Susannah read:

> While an intrinsic ardor prompts to write
> The Muses promise to assist my pen.
> 'Twas not long since I left my native shore,
> The land of errors and Egyptian gloom:
> Father of mercy! 'twas thy gracious hand
> Brought me in safety from those dark abodes.

"She actually wrote this?"

John shrugged. "She claims to have. I assumed she had copied it. I came across it in the library. Apparently she dropped it, and when I showed it to her she said she had written it herself."

"Mary told me she had been attempting to write verse, but I never took her seriously."

"She said she admired Pope's work so much she wanted to write something herself."

"And what did you say to that?"

"Just what I would any servant. Tend to your chores and forget such foolishness."

"John Wheatley, you didn't . . ."

His eyebrows shot up at the vehemence in her voice. After a moment he said in an indulgent tone, "My dear Susannah, I know how taken you are with Phillis. Granted, she's an appealing little tyke, but her skin is black. Once and for all, I expect you to see she stays in her place."

"Place?" Susannah exploded. "Just what is her place?" Suddenly all the years of sitting in the Wheeler family pew listening to the Reverend Cotton Mather thunder from the pulpit, "Christian love knows no bounds," welled up inside Susannah. "The child has a mind," she said sharply, "and I cannot in good conscience stop her from making use of it." She loosened her hair and let it fall to her shoulders. "I remember well the Reverend Mather saying it was only the skin not the mind which differs in color. Look at Mr. Occom. His skin is not white. Tell me, Mr. Wheatley, is it wrong for him to read and do the Lord's work?"

But John was not to be put off. "I wonder," he said, "if you are not making the mistake of seeing in Phillis what you once hoped our Mary might be."

So she had not managed to hide it from him after all. And if he knew that, he must know too that her hopes for Mary had been a projection of what she had once hoped for herself. She kept her eyes averted as she brushed her hair. How well she understood Phillis' thirst for knowledge. How many times as a child had she longed to be as free as her brothers, to get out from under, first a father, then a husband who, no matter how kind, controlled every moment of her life. She could still recall the day the twins were born. For such a short time they were truly equal; but by the time they learned to walk, Mary was patterned to be docile and domestic like her mother, although those who said it little dreamed how dissatisfied Susannah was with the role she was expected to play. Somehow, some way, she had vowed as she fed, bathed, and diapered her only daughter, Mary would have the same opportunity to learn, to grow, and to experience life as Nat.

But Mary had wanted nothing more than to follow the image that her mother showed the world. It was not what Susannah secretly aspired for her daughter. Glimpses of anything else only brought an exasperated, "Oh, Mother." Mary preferred needlework to books. She went to school only because her grandmother told her a bit of culture was essential to the shaping of a lady. Susannah raised her eyes to look at John. It was hard to know if he suspected the truth, and she could not bring herself to discuss it with him.

She was suddenly ashamed of her outburst. After all, he was a good man and she was his wife, bound by the vow of obedience she had taken. "I can't deny I'm proud of Phillis," she said slowly. "No matter where I go everyone I meet wants to know what she has learned this week. Surely you would not want me to hide her accomplishments? And besides," she smiled, "you must admit the religious training I have given her has not been in vain. See, right here she speaks of "my heavenly father." At any rate, I think she will be spending less time at her studies. Mary grows weary of teaching."

"Just as well," John said. "I should rather see Mary pay more attention to the young men who come calling."

CHAPTER VI

By August it was obvious how Boston felt about the Stamp Act. Everywhere there was talk about how unfair it was, the prevailing opinion, "If we stand for this, what's next?"

The deed was done during the night. Early risers walking past the huge elm tree on Boylston Avenue were shocked to see an effigy of Andrew Oliver, Royal Secretary of the province and brother-in-law of Lieutenant Governor Thomas Hutchinson. It was the people's answer to the Stamp Act, for Oliver was in charge of the stamps due to arrive any day. All day people walked by and stared at the likeness. No one laughed or smiled. They just stared.

Nerves grew taut. Just before dark a crowd gathered near the tree, then marched on to the new stamp office and Oliver's home. Both were destroyed by dawn. Even the plants in Oliver's garden were uprooted as the crowd added the final touch by lighting a bonfire on the front lawn and burning him in effigy. He resigned his post the next day.

"This is just the beginning, and God help us all if it doesn't stop," Nat said that night at supper.

Oliver out of the way, the Lieutenant Governor became the next target as the mob appeared nightly under his window to demand he state he had never supported the Stamp Act. But Hutchinson said nothing.

"Why doesn't the man defend himself?" Susannah asked. "Everyone knows he spoke out against it. After all, it's his job to enforce the law whether he likes it or not."

"Unfortunately, those people don't think rationally," Nat said. "They need a scapegoat, and Hutchinson's it. You can bet Sam Adams is in back of this. He hates Hutchinson."

Phillis awakened abruptly in the early morning hours of the twenty-sixth. Someone was trying to break into the house. She ran to the window and looked out. She could see nothing, but she heard shouting and strange noises from the north end of town. Back in bed she buried her head under the covers, sleeping in fits and starts until dawn.

It was midmorning before they learned a mob had stormed the cellar of one of the custom houses and broken open some barrels of rum. Then, roaring drunk, the unruly crowd marched on Hutchinson's palatial home overlooking Fish Street.

"There's nothing left but a shell . . ." Master John's voice carried to where Phillis was sorting clothes. "Those animals took axes and smashed everything—chandeliers—furniture— they even tore off the roof." His voice rose. "By God, if I could get my hands on those bastards for just five minutes . . ."

"Was anyone hurt?" Miss Susannah's voice was strained.

"I hear Hutchinson and the girls barely escaped with their lives. They say he has nothing left but the clothes on his back. Everything he's worked for gone in a few hours." Master John's voice broke. "It's unbelievable."

From the shadows of her mind came a long forgotten sensation of horror such as Phillis had never known. She shivered. What was hidden there was buried, but she knew it was closely aligned with what was happening in the streets.

September and October passed with no further demonstrations. On November first, the day the Stamp Act took effect, the funeral bells tolled while flags flew at half mast. People slept fitfully, expecting the worst. But nothing happened. As the month wore on, the rebellion they feared failed to materialize. The Stamp Act was simply ignored. Newspapers were sent out without stamps, the courts closed, and business came to a standstill, leaving the stamp agents with nothing to do. As the new year came and went, everyone congratulated themselves on so successfully outwitting the Parliament. Parliament was collecting no money from them, they said jubilantly. They, the King's subjects, had managed to have the last word, confirmed the first week in May when a ship sailed into Boston's port with the news that Parliament had repealed the Stamp Act.

Boston reacted like a mare let loose in a pasture. All that night and the next day her people worked feverishly getting ready for the greatest celebration Boston had ever seen. On the Common, a huge pyramid made of oiled paper took shape. Hung with lanterns it would be paraded through the streets like a giant torch.

The peal of bells, then the boom of cannon from Castle Island, followed by return salutes from ships anchored in the harbor awakened the Wheatleys before dawn the next day. The whole town was like a carnival as musicians roamed through the streets playing fifes and drums under windows. Lamps blinked on in one house after another as people dressed and prepared to join the revellers.

Phillis was overjoyed when Master John gave all the servants permission to join the festivities. "Stay with Mary, Phillis," he cautioned. "Otherwise your mistress will worry."

She had never seen so many people in one place as they joined the crowds surging up Cornhill Street. Today there was no master or mistress as everyone—schoolchildren, town officials, apprentices, slaves—all joined together as one to express their common joy.

By the time they finally returned home, the first bonfires were already being lit on the Common, and from the huge elm in Hanover Square, now called the Liberty Tree, three hundred lanterns glowed softly in the gathering dusk.

After supper, Susannah sent Phillis to help Mary dress for the party John Hancock was hosting in his hilltop mansion. Her excitement was tempered by a sudden flash of envy as she adjusted the pan hoops and slipped the green velvet frock over Mary's blonde head. It wasn't fair. White people got to do everything. Would she ever be free to do as she wanted? Or would she always belong to someone? For some inexplicable reason, a vision of Mr. Occom flashed before her. He didn't have white skin, but he wore fine clothes. Right now he was in London meeting with people in the King's cabinet. She felt a surge of hope. If an Indian could live like that, perhaps one day she might enjoy privileges also.

"Phillis..." Mary sounded exasperated. "You're a million miles away."

"What?"

"I said get a needle and thread. This button is loose. You didn't even hear me. What were you thinking so hard about?"

"Nothing," said Phillis as she sewed on the button and began to lace up the satin stomacher embroidered with blue flowers and studded with seed pearls. Just this once she wished she could wear something besides black with a white apron. She adjusted the modesty piece so that it revealed just a hint of Mary's soft swelling bosom, conscious she herself would soon be able to show one off to good advantage should she ever have the chance.

She went to her room as soon as Mary left. From her window she watched bonfires shoot sparks high into the air. The moonlight gave a pearl-like texture to roofs and steeples as fireworks rose and exploded into a myriad of multi-colored sparks. Boston was ecstatic.

Almost without realizing it, Phillis picked up paper and quill, and dipped it into the well and began doodling. *King,* she wrote, encircling the word with a crownlike drawing. *Crown on his head,* she scrawled underneath.

Before she knew it the words began to take shape as thoughts unexpressed throughout this tumultous day found their way onto the paper.

From out of the many books she had read leaped the right words.

Halfway through she stopped. Master John had reprimanded her for wasting time writing poetry. But could he object when she was in her own room at this time of night? She was oblivious to anything but the scene below as she wrote, pondered, scratched out a line, rewrote, and finally she was finished.

As she read it over, a glimmer of a daring idea surfaced in her mind. Should she send it to the King? She rejected the idea as preposterous and laid the paper on her desk, but after a moment's hesitation took out a fresh sheet.

She copied the lines she had just written, then stopped. How did one go about sending his Majesty a letter? She thought a moment, wrote, "To the King's Most Excellent Majesty, George III, London, England," then rummaged in her drawer for sealing wax.

That done, she undressed and blew out the candle. The noise of the revellers still reverberated in her ears as she pulled the bedcurtains shut.

CHAPTER VII

1767 14 yrs old

EUPHORIC WAS THE WORD FOR BOSTON following
the repeal of the Stamp Act. It was a time when radicals found
it virtually impossible to rally anyone to the Patriot cause.
The people's protests had been heeded. Once again they
looked to England as a beloved protector, realizing it was
her armed might that was powerful enough to keep any outside power, particularly France, from sweeping down out of
Canada and usurping England's hold on the New World.

But such things were of no concern to Phillis as she
stretched her mind in new studies, wrote poetry in the pri-
vacy of her room, spent pleasant hours reading to Susannah,
and coped with physical changes. At thirteen, she was rapidly
leaving childhood behind. Tall and slender, there was an
aristocratic look about her, the promise of beauty she had
shown as a child blossoming into reality.

"Looks to me like we got bait for the young bucks," Dora
commented one afternoon as a squeaky-voiced boy delivered
groceries. "Used to be I carried 'em home myself." She
grinned. "You should've seen his face yesterday when he
came while Phillis was out with Miss Mary."

Phillis pretended not to have heard, but she felt herself flush. She had no idea how to handle such talk. Nor did she know what to do about the sidelong glances from the boys in church, the unrepeatable words whispered just loud enough for her to catch as she passed the livery stable around the corner. Instinctively, she knew it was somehow connected to her monthly periods, but how she did not understand. If only she had a mother, but she could never bring herself to discuss such things with Miss Susannah. It was Sukey to whom she had run at the first bloodstains on her underdrawers, convinced she had contracted some fatal disease.

"Nothin' to worry about, child, you're just growin' up," Sukey reassured her. "You're growin' into a woman, and one day you'll be snugglin' up to a man in bed just like everyone else." She put her arm around Phillis. "Don't look like that. There ain't nothin' better on a cold night."

But Phillis knew if she ever did, it would be with none of the gawky boys who lived in the neighborhood. Young as she was, she knew a man would have to offer her a lot more than his body. Not one boy she knew could even read or write his name. If only they were like the gentlemen who came to call on Miss Mary. They never jostled themselves against her like Willie tried to do. Instead they brought Mary a book or a bouquet of flowers, and they went for walks.

But she kept her thoughts to herself. Being different caused enough problems.

At least she was proving her worth to Master John. Although she never said a word about her fears, she knew slaves could be sold. Hadn't Hannah, who belonged on the next street been traded off for a man? Even though Sukey assured her Master John considered them part of the family, Phillis planned on taking no chances. Since that first time she had heard Master John complain, she had been careful never to let him catch her reading a book or even writing one word on a piece of paper. From Sukey she had learned how to fold and put away his clothes. Her efforts were bearing fruit. She had overheard him say to Susannah. "I do believe Phillis is proving a worthwhile investment after all. My drawers have never looked neater. And she does make a respectable toddy."

But only a few days later, there was a decided edge to his voice as he summoned her to the parlor where Mary and Susannah were seated on the sofa with their needlework. Mary looked puzzled, Susannah grave.

"I had a caller this afternoon, Phillis," Master John began abruptly. "A Mr. Josiah Greenwood stopped by with an incredible story."

Greenwood, Phillis knew, was a minor town official, but what had this to do with her? She grew apprehensive as Master John held out a letter and said, "He brought me this. He also told me a servant in my household was supposed to have written it, and you are the only one here who writes poetry."

Phillis' heart pounded. It was her verse. She could tell by the spacing of the words.

Mary voiced the question. "Where did Mr. Greenwood get this?"

"It seems the King of England received it some time ago and had instructed Lord Dartmouth of the Royal Court to send this copy to the governor. The story Josiah brought me is that it was written by Phillis Wheatley."

He handed Phillis the letter.

At sight of the words "To the King's Most Excellent Majesty" she thought back to that night in her room after the repeal of the Stamp Act. Her voice was barely audible as she forced herself to look at Master John.

"Yes, I wrote it. But I meant no harm."

"I am sure she didn't," said Susannah. "Let me see it."

Phillis listened as Susannah read aloud;

> Your subjects hope, dread Sire,
> The crown upon your brows may flourish long,
> And that your arm may in your God be strong!
> O, may your sceptre numerous nations sway,
> And all with love and readiness obey.
> But how shall we the British king reward?
> Rule thou in peace, our father and our lord!
> 'Midst the remembrance of thy favors past,
> The meanest peasants most admire the last.
> May George, beloved by all the nations round,
> Live with Heaven's choicest, constant blessings crowned.
> Great God! direct and guard him from on high,
> And from his head let every evil fly;
> And may each clime with equal gladness see
> A monarch's smile can set his subjects free.

"Phillis, this is beautiful. When did you write it?"

"The night of the celebration. I sent it to England the next day."

"But why didn't you tell us?" Mary's eyes sparkled. "I think it's marvellous. The King receiving a letter from a . . ."

"Mary," Susannah cut her off.

"It's all right, Miss Susannah. I am a slave. It's not fitting I write to His Majesty."

Mary tossed her head. "Who cares? I'd like to have seen the King's face when he read it."

Master John frowned. "The problem is, Phillis, no one believes you wrote it."

Of course, Phillis thought resentfully. Who ever expected a slave to be capable of anything?

"Does it really matter?" Mary asked.

"Apparently it does to the King. Lord Dartmouth, on behalf of the King has sent instructions to the governor to find out who this Phillis Wheatley is, and if she is a servant, how she can be capable of writing something like this." A smile touched the corners of Master John's mouth. "It would seem our Phillis has brought notoriety to our usually staid house."

"Anyone'll believe it once they hear Phillis talk," said Mary. "The King has probably never heard of a slave who can read, let alone write."

"How does the King propose to find out if this is actually Phillis' work?" Susannah asked.

"I understand he has instructed the governor to appoint a commission to look into the matter. That's what brought Josiah here. He says they have called a committee of eighteen prominent citizens together for the purpose of examining her."

"Oh, no," Phillis protested.

"I have been appointed to it myself. I shall be with you every minute," he said.

"When am I to meet them?"

"They have asked that you be ready a week from tomorrow." Master John smiled. "Don't worry about it. I am convinced you are equal to anything they ask of you."

As she left the room, Phillis had the distinct impression that for the first time her master was proud of her.

"Well, Mrs. Wheatley," he was saying, "It seems we have something more than we bargained for . . ."

Phillis was up before dawn on the appointed day, leafing through her books and papers as the first streaks of dawn lightened the sky, already in the kitchen when the others arrived to start breakfast.

"Land sakes, I've never seen anyone so jumpy. Here, eat something," Sukey commanded, but Phillis was unable to swallow a bite. Her stomach felt like it did the time she ate unripe fruit. Pushing the food away, she settled for sips of tea.

"You have nothing to worry about," Mary assured her as Master John called it was time to leave.

"I wish you could go with me," Phillis said. "I'm frightened."

"You don't need me." Mary smiled. "You'll do just fine, won't she, Nat?"

"I am sure of it, but just in case . . ." He pressed something into Phillis' palm. "Not that you'll need this."

She felt her eyes mist as she gazed down at his good luck medallion. "Thank you," she said softly.

She picked up her shawl and started downstairs where Susannah was waiting beside the front door. "Remember, all things are possible through Him who strengthens us," she quoted softly as she kissed Phillis' cheek.

She could have sworn it was hours instead of minutes before Master John led her up the steps of the State House and through the spacious hall to the council chambers. Her knees were weak and her mouth felt as parched as though she hadn't had water in days. If only she could turn and run before that door opened, but Master John's firm grip on her hand restrained her.

Inside they stood before a huge table around which sat seventeen men, all looking at Phillis.

"Good morning, Your Excellency, gentlemen," Master John bowed. "May I present Phillis."

The man at the head of the table rose and bowed slightly. "Come, sit down, Phillis, Mr. Wheatley."

So this was Governor Hutchinson. No wonder they called him "Tommy Skin and Bones." Long lean body, long nose, long slender hands with extraordinarily long, narrow thumbs. The mark of an aristocrat was stamped on every feature, but she knew the moment she looked into his soft hazel eyes that he was a kind, compassionate man.

An aide pulled out a chair. She sat down gingerly, wishing fervently she could become invisible. It was as though a hammer beat at the back of her head. She would never be able to think of a single answer.

"I understand you have written His Majesty a most unusual letter," Hutchinson began.

"Yes, sir. I did."

"His Majesty has understandably expressed some doubt this poem is yours, Phillis; however, your master assures me it is. Tell me, can you recite it from memory for us?"

"Your subjects hope, dread sire, the crown upon your head may flourish long . . ." Thank heaven they had asked her something she needn't think about. She noted how attentive they became as all the lines rolled effortlessly off her tongue. When she had finished the fifteen lines, Hutchinson smiled.

"A beautiful piece of work. I have no doubt it is your creation. How else could you have recited it so fluently and with such feeling?"

"Thank you." She began to relax.

"Who is your tutor?" Hutchinson inquired.

"I have learned from Miss Mary and Mr. Nathaniel, sir, along with the many books in my master's library."

So skillfully she hardly realized it, Hutchinson led her into a discussion of what she had learned. She was astonished to find the questions easy to answer. Many were from the Bible, familiar territory for her. From there they led into Astronomy, History, and Literature, and Latin.

"Whom do you rate as the greatest of the Latin poets?" Andrew Oliver asked in precise, clipped tones.

She felt herself tense. "Rome produced several, but the greatest was Ovid."

"Can you give us an example?" The gentleman who asked the question looked skeptical. He had appeared bored through most of the interview. Phillis searched her memory. *I must get this right*, she thought as she saw Master John nod silently, his face radiating confidence.

> "*Nec tibi directes placeat via quinquae per arcus, Sectus in obliqum est late curvemine lines, Zenarumque trium contentus fine pelumque, Effugit astralem iuntamque aquinonibus Arcton.*"

The words flowed freely, and she could not resist casting a triumphant glance at the little man who scowled and drummed his fingers on the table. When she had finished, he turned to the man next to him.

"Can't possibly understand ... slave ..." his whisper carried so that Phillis clearly heard the words.

Hutchinson's eyes lighted. "Ah, the Metamorphosis. Can you translate that for us, Phillis?"

She took a deep breath and said a small prayer. Hutchinson was considered the foremost translator in the colonies. She dare not make a mistake. Her palms grew clammy as she began;

> "*And do not take the way straight across the five zones. The path is cut obliquely in a wide curve and contained within the boundary of the three inner zones. It avoids the South Pole and the North with its winds.*"

Every eye was on her as she finished. This time she didn't mind. The acclaim in their eyes gave her a heady feeling she had never experienced before as they began to clap in unison.

"Excellent ... phenomenal ..."

"Beautiful, Phillis." Hutchinson clasped her hand as the body dissolved into informality, everyone crowding around her. Questions were flung at her, and she entered into the discussions eagerly. Master John beamed.

Hutchinson pounded the table with his gavel. "Order, gentlemen. There is one more item of business we must attend to. May we have a motion to the effect we certify we are satisfied as to Phillis' intellectual capacities?"

"So moved."

"I second."

"It has been moved and seconded. All in favor say aye."

The ayes resounded through the room. Hutchinson turned to Phillis. "I shall have a paper drawn up for all to see, and a copy dispatched immediately to the King." His eyes twinkled. "Now what do you think of that?"

"Oh, thank you sir, Thank you all."

"And how do you propose to use this knowledge you have acquired?"

Phillis turned and recognized the popular John Hancock. Dressed in a suit of royal blue velvet, lace ruffles at the neck and below the sleeves of his coat, his waistcoat a brilliant scarlet satin, he obviously enjoyed being conspicuous. Not that he needed elaborate dress to be noticed. Never had she seen a more handsome man.

"I mean to use my education the best I can to further the cause of God and my country," she answered.

"Admirable," said Hancock.

It was as though she had been transformed into one of the goddesses out of mythology when she and Master John left some time later. She ran the last block home, "Prince, I answered every question," she cried.

Prince's face was a wreath of smiles. "I told everyone you'd do just fine. I said they ain't nobody as smart as our Phillis." He immediately glanced apprehensively at Master John as he realized what his words implied.

"That's quite all right, Prince. I, too, am proud of her."

Instinct told Phillis this experience marked a turning point in her life, although she had no idea what form it would take.

Thomas Hutchinson, Royal Governor of the Massachusetts Colony and the seventeen judges in attendance affixed their signature to a drawn affidavit that was intended to impress the most skeptical members of the community.

TO THE PUBLIC

As it has been repeatedly suggested to the Publisher, by persons who have seen the Manuscript, that numbers would be ready to suspect they were not really the writings of Phillis, he has procured the following Attestation, from the most respectable characters in Boston, that none might have the least ground for disputing their original:

We, whose names are under-written, do assure the World, that the Poems specified in the following page* were (as we verily believe) written by Phillis, a young Negro girl, who was but a few years since brought an uncultivated barbarian from Africa, and has ever since been, and now is, under the disadvantage of serving as a slave in a family in this Town. She has been examined by some of the best judges, and is thought qualified to write them. Behold the prophet in his towering flight!

The Hon. Andrew Oliver, *Lieutenant Governor,*
His Excellency, Thomas Hutchison, *Governor,*

The Hon. Thomas Hubbard,	The Rev. Matthew Byles, D.D.
The Hon. John Erving,	The Rev. Edw'd Pemberton,
The Hon. James Pitts,	D.D.
The Hon. Harrison Gray,	The Rev. Andrew Elliot, D.D.
The Hon. James Bowdoin	The Rev. Samuel Cooper, D.D.
John Hancock, Esq.	The Rev. Mr. Samuel Mather,
Joseph Green, Esq.	The Rev. Mr. John Moorhead,
Richard Carey, Esq.	Mr. John Wheatley, (her
The Rev. Charles Chauncey,	Master.)
D.D.	

N. B. The original Attestation, signed by the above Gentlemen, may be seen by applying to Archibald Bell, Bookseller, No. 8, Aldgate Street.

In addition to the signatures of the 17 men, John Wheatley, her master also appended his signature with an added note that read:

> "Phillis was brought from Africa to America in the Year 1761, between seven and eight years of Age. Without any assistance from School Education, and by only what she was taught in the Family, she, in sixteen Months Time from her Arrival, attained the English Language, to which she was an utter stranger before, to such a degree as to read any of the most difficult Parts of the Sacred Writings, to the astonishment of all who heard her.
>
> As to her Writing, her own Curiousity, led her to it; and this she learnt in so short a Time, that in the year 1765, she wrote a letter to the Rev. Mr. Occum, the Indian Minister, while in England.

She has a great inclination to learn the Latin Tongue, and has made some progress in it.

This Relation is given by her Master, who bought her, and with whom she now lives.

John Wheatley (signed)

CHAPTER VIII

BY NIGHTFALL, most all of the community had heard of Phillis' appearance before the King's Committee. Reactions were varied, and although the majority were favorable, there were detractors.

But for the most part, Phillis' accomplishments elevated her to the status of a minor celebrity. People who had once virtually ignored her now seemed genuinely interested in what she was doing. She was thrilled to have the Reverend Mr. Mather, who had been among the members of the committee, loan her books from his impressive library, said to be one of the finest in the colonies.

But along with this fame came a feeling she was nothing more than a prize monkey on the end of a rope, expected to come forth with bits of verse whenever she and Susannah chanced to meet someone in the street.

The boys no longer lingered beside her at church either. Not that there was much chance, for the moment she arrived she was engulfed by Susannah's friends.

Susannah was concerned too, but for a far different reason. She had hoped Phillis would outgrow her tendency to take ill at the slightest provocation; but lately, long after the family had retired, her coughing kept them awake.

"She must save her strength to use her talents as God intended her to," Susannah maintained. "I won't have her taxing her energy doing tasks any ordinary servant is fitted for when she could be spending the time at her studies."

"I wonder if we've done right by her," Master John mused when Susannah told him she had instructed Dora and Sukey not to expect Phillis to help with breakfast.

"What do you mean by that?" Susannah's tone was sharp.

"All this studying. I wonder if she wouldn't be happier living like other slaves do."

Susannah's chin jutted forward. "She'd have been dead by now," she snapped. "You know she's too fragile for hard work."

"Taxing the brain can be just as hard on a person." He raised his eyes to hers. "I just wonder who is receiving the benefit of all this."

"Why, she is. How can you ask a question like that?"

"I wonder." He looked at her a moment, then said, "Of course, we did buy her for your sake, so if it makes you happy to indulge her I suppose she has served her purpose."

Susannah looked at him sharply, but he had already buried his head in the account book. She smiled.

Seldom did a day pass without Phillis writing new verse, most of it long after the rest of the household had retired. Strange, but it was almost as though the mere act of disrobing, blowing out the candle, and climbing under the covers signalled the beginning of the creative process for her. No matter how she put her mind to it at a more reasonable hour, it was invariably as she lay there, that she experienced her most prolific time, when snatches of verse formed effortlessly in her mind. Too weary to even think of getting up to write them down, she would vow to remember them in the morning only to find the once vivid passages gone, her mind blank.

Gradually she learned to get up, relight the candle, and capture the words as they came.

The family became increasingly indulgent, often letting her stay in bed long after the others had gone about their daily routine. "Leave her be," Susannah would say. "She needs her rest."

More time to write meant less time to spend in the supportive fellowship of the other slaves. Not that Phillis enjoyed household tasks, but there was an accepting "all barriers down" feeling when they worked together in the kitchen. Now that had been snatched away, and in her loneliness, she turned even more to her books and her poetry.

It was late that summer when Master John told them about meeting a Mr. Tanner from Newport.

"It seems he was here on business and heard of Phillis," he told Susannah and Phillis as they sat sewing lace edging on pillow cases. He has a slave girl he thinks may have come from Africa on the same ship as Phillis. Nothing positive, but it is something I should like to look into. Tanner says his bill of sale is dated June, 1761, same as mine."

Phillis felt first disbelief, then wonder. Would this girl know her?

Susannah peered at her anxiously. "Do you remember anything at all about the voyage?" she asked.

"Only that I was cold and hungry when I got here."

"You recall none of the others with you?"

"No. Nothing."

Master John continued. "The girl's name is Obour. Tanner says she is older than Phillis, twenty or twenty one now." He paused. "I have to go to Newport soon on business. I have a mind to look in on the family. Frankly, I don't think it should concern us, but Tanner seems anxious to know if they might recognize each other. He says Obour is a bright girl. Still talks about her past, seems to feel the need to contact someone from her former life."

Long after she had gone to bed, Phillis lay shaken by the news. If she saw this girl, would it awaken memories long dormant? Did she really want to remember? For the first time, she tried desperately to recall something, anything. Why, she had parents the same color as she, yet until now she had never really thought about them. Who was the woman who had given birth to her? Did she have brothers and sisters? What were they like? Were they still alive? Did she look like any of them? They must have given her a name. What was it? What had her early life been like? The questions kaleidoscoped in her mind. She had read a little about Africa. The dark continent. A vast land about which so little was known. Never once had she admitted its being a part of her heritage until now. Her mind raced as she pondered the unanswered questions. It was like tracing a spring . . . a vision of bubbling water sprang into her mind as fragments of phrases began to form in her mind. Rising, she did not even stop to light a candle, relying only on the moonlight as she dipped her quill into inkwell and began to write:

> ————— Inspire ye sacred mine
> Your vent'rous Africa in her great design
> Mneme, immortal pow'r, I trace my springs:
> Assist my strains while I thy glories sing.

Pen in midair, she stopped. Would this Obour Tanner be able to tell her anything about her origins? *Please, God, I have to know.*

Never had she known time to pass so agonizingly slow as when Master John was in Newport. He returned late one afternoon, and all through supper she struggled to hide her impatience.

Why was he deliberately prolonging the suspense? Everytime there was a pause in the conversation Mary would ask some ridiculous question like, were the women wearing the same hoops they did in Boston? And nothing would do but he must give Nat a complete rundown on the newly passed Townshend acts imposing stiff tariffs on imported goods. Phillis began to despair of his ever getting around to what she wanted to know, when he finally turned to her and said, "I have met this young woman and talked with her at length. She is a remarkable person and claims to remember you." He smiled. "I have every reason to believe you were both on the same ship."

Phillis closed her eyes, praying for some image to form, but there was nothing. "Are you sure?" she asked. Since he had first mentioned meeting Tanner the yearning to see someone who shared her beginnings had grown more intense with each day.

"She described you in detail as you were when your mistress and I first saw you," he said, then added, "Mrs. Tanner has asked that you accompany your mistress to Newport so that you and Obour can meet." He finished the last of his tea. "Your mistress is already making plans. Calls it the perfect excuse for a holiday."

Phillis found it hard to believe, but there was confirmation in Susannah's eyes as she smiled and said, "We will leave early next week. Obour is just as anxious to see you as I can see you are to meet her."

They were to travel by coach. Sukey immediately set to work readying their travel clothes and preparing food which would withstand the humid weather, although Susannah assured her they would have no need for it, since they would stop at inns along the way.

The stage was to call for them at three in the morning, Susannah told her the day before departure.

Phillis heard it the moment it stopped under their window. It was still dark when she and Susannah climbed into the coach.

"Move to the back," the gravel-voiced driver called as they scrambled awkwardly over the backless benches transversing the coach. There were only two other passengers when they boarded, but by the time they reached the town gates it was filled to its capacity of ten.

Phillis was much too excited to care that she was squeezed into a corner, her feet propped on baggage stowed under the seat. She was thankful it was necessary to stop and refresh the horses every ten to twelve miles. By the beginning of the second day, Phillis had learned the best place to sit was the middle of the bench, for the only way to keep the coach from overturning when it hit a rut was for them all to lean to the opposite side and heaven help the person on the end.

Despite the jolts, the aching muscles, and the claustrophobic cramming of so many into such close quarters, inconveniences notwithstanding, Phillis loved every minute of the journey through the gently rollings hills with pretty towns nestled in the valleys.

Every joint was stiff by the time they reached Newport, and fatigue had deepened the lines around Susannah's mouth. At the inn where Master John had arranged for them to stay, Phillis opened the window and leaned out to take a deep breath of the tangy salt air. Her excitement was tempered with anxiety. How would the meeting go tomorrow?

The big clapboard house, set back from the road on a knoll, was visible long before they turned into the driveway in their rented carriage. Even the door was impressive, intricately paneled with a circular fanlight at the top. Phillis hoped the carved pineapple above it, the traditional sign of hospitality, was a good omen. She felt much as she had that morning she went to the State House with Master John. Susannah lifted the ornate brass knocker.

"I am Mrs. Wheatley, and I have brought Phillis," Susannah told the black man who opened the door.

His teeth flashed in a wide grin. "Come right in. Mis' Tanner been looking for you." He ushered them into the parlor.

Seated on the high backed love seat, Phillis looked around

with interest. The expensive looking flowered wallpaper, the fine grained panelling over the fireplace, the oriental rug underfoot, and the elegant Queen Anne chairs all spoke of quality, but the room lacked warmth. The stiffly hanging drapes were of a heavy lustreless material, dark brown in color, and from the wall hung a row of portraits, stern-faced, as though humor was an unknown quality.

The woman's skirts rustled as she floated into the room. "Mistress Wheatley, I'm Sarah Tanner. Such a pleasure to meet you." She kissed Susannah on the cheek and bade her be seated. Behind her stood a tall black girl. Her dress was similar to the one Phillis wore, but the material was of lesser quality. Her skin was a trifle darker than Phillis', her cheeks round and full, mouth wide and full lipped. Her eyes were kind, yet sad, as though bitter memories were hidden in their depths.

"And this must be Phillis." Mrs. Tanner took Phillis' trembling hand in her soft pudgy one.

Phillis' hand remained in Mrs. Tanner's, but her eyes were on the girl.

"Yes, I know you," Obour said slowly. "You're the child I held in my arms. They said you were dying that last night out." Her gentle voice was low pitched.

"I don't really remember you," Phillis murmured as they embraced. "I don't remember anything."

"You coughed so much you couldn't keep any food down. Everyone said you would never live long enough to be sold."

"She looked half starved when we saw her in the marketplace," Susannah said softly. "I shall never forget it."

"The Lord meant you should live," said Obour.

She's a Christian too. Phillis immediately felt a kinship she had never experienced before.

"Would you like to see my garden, Mrs. Wheatley?" their hostess asked, breaking the silence. "My roses took first prize. . . ." she said as the two went out toward the garden.

"Do you remember anything about our homeland?" Phillis asked as soon as the two girls were alone.

"Of course. It was beautiful. I come from a big family. At night I can still see my brothers going with my father to hunt, and my mother, grandmother, sisters, and I going out to pick berries." Her dark eyes glowed with memories. "And I remember how blue the sky, how high the grass grew . . ." Her voice throbbed. "I was loved. I shall never forget that once I was loved." The light suddenly went out of her eyes. "Before the slave traders."

"My family?" Phillis' voice was tremulous. "Did you know them?"

Obour shook her head. "We came from so many villages. I don't recall ever seeing you until after we were on the boat." She paused. "I'm not surprised you remember nothing. You never said a word the whole journey. We wondered if you had ever learned to talk."

"I only wish I could remember something."

"Be thankful you don't." The gentle voice had turned bitter. "The Lord must have wanted you to forget. I only wish I could." She paused. "We were in tight pack. Do you know what that means?"

Phillis shook her head.

"They pack as many as they can into the space. So what if more die that way? It's how many get across that counts. Each one is worth money. Would you like to remember what it's like to lie in your own filth?" She shuddered. "I shall never forget it."

Her eyes flashed. "Your being sick was a blessing. But for that you'd have been taken to the sailors' deck just like the rest of us. Night after night, three or four of them one right after the other. I can still feel their sweaty bodies on top of me, their hands on my breasts, between my legs, their stinking breath in my face."

She took a deep breath. "Forgive me," she said, her voice

gentle again. "I've upset you. Let us speak of more pleasant things. Tell me about your family. Your master speaks of you with so much pride. He says you have even studied Latin."

Phillis was amazed how easy it was to talk to Obour. Years of pent-up feelings poured out as she told about Nat and Mary, Sukey, Dora, and Prince. "I know I'm in probably the best home any slave could possibly have, but . . ."

"There's something wrong," Obour finished for her.

Phillis nodded. "I can't explain it."

"I can." Again Obour's eyes flashed with anger. "You're not free just as I'm not free, and Phillis, nothing—not a good home nor a full belly or book learning will ever make up for the fact we can never go where we want or do what we want. Even the poorest white who can't read a single word out of a book has something we can only dream about. His life is his own." She lowered her voice. "Not that I let my mistress hear me talk like this. She and the master have treated me well. I do little besides look after the children. It's a pleasant job, and like you, my master has permitted me to learn to read and write, although I shall never be able to do the things you have."

"I often wonder why I have been given so much more than other slaves," Phillis murmured.

"Be thankful to the Lord for the opportunity. So few of us are ever given a chance to learn anything. Most white people think a dark skin means we were born without brains. And if we do manage to learn, it can lead to trouble. I know slaves who were sold when their masters discovered they could read."

"But why?"

"Because they fear if too many of us learn anything we will turn against them."

Before Phillis could phrase an answer Obour added, "And someday we will."

"If only you lived in Boston," she said to Obour. In just

this short time it was as though the two had known each other a lifetime. Fond as she was of Dora and Sukey, she could never feel this close to either of them.

"Distance need be no barrier to friendship," Obour said. "We can write letters."

"I'd like that. And you can come to Boston sometime."

"Perhaps, if the Lord wills it," Obour replied. She smiled. "But let's not talk of separation. My mistress has kindly given me the entire day to do as I please." They left the house and walked slowly to the shore.

Never had Phillis known a day to pass more quickly. For the first time in years she felt total acceptance. "I'm so glad we found each other," she said late that afternoon as they walked barefoot along the shore.

"I, too, little friend." Obour's voice was thick with emotion.

Before she and Susannah left the next day, Phillis gave Obour a copy of the poem she had stayed up to write the night before.

> " 'Twas mercy brought me from my pagan land
> Taught my benighted soul to understand
> That there's a God, that there's a Savior too.
> Once I redemption neither sought nor knew
> Some view our sable race with scornful eye:
> "Their color is a diabolic dye."
> Remember, Christians, Negros, black as Cain,
> May be refined and join the angelic train."

CHAPTER IX

1770

BACK IN BOSTON, her studies and chores, and corresponding with Obour, her new friend, kept Phillis so busy she paid little heed to what was being termed "the change in Mary."

Sukey glowed with pride. "My baby's in love. 'Bout time too. Thought she'd be spoken for long before now. Just as well she waited, though. She'd be hard put to find a much better catch than a clergyman, 'specially one as nice as this one."

The object of Mary's affections was the newly ordained young pastor of North Church, John Lathrop. Three years older than Mary's twenty seven, he was handsome with his straight nose, deep set dark eyes, and sensitive mouth.

Only Susannah was not surprised. She had suspected some time ago it might be John Lathrop rather than the church itself when Mary asked her father's permission to attend North Church. "After all," Mary had said demurely when it looked as though he was about to refuse, "it was Mother's church until she married you."

"I personally don't think much of their hellfire and brimstone preaching," he had replied, "although I can't say it did your Mother any lasting harm. You may attend Old North two Sundays a month, but the other two as well as midweek you will attend King's Chapel with us as usual." He shook his head. "That's the trouble with you young folks. No sense of what the Lord meant you to do. He meant families to worship together, not scattered all over town."

Mr. Lathrop's conscientiousness about paying calls on his new part-time parishoner soon became the talk of the household.

The whole town nodded approval. The young pastor was gaining a respected place in the community and needed a wife. By the winter, all Boston knew he had won the hand of Mary Wheatley. In February they announced their intent to wed. But the news was overshadowed by what happened a mere fortnight later.

It had been three years since the passage of the Townshend Acts which levied taxes on such things as paint, paper, glass, and worst of all tea, the mainstay of every New England household; and while there had been no actual rebellion, there were sporadic incidents organized by the Sons of Liberty: customs officials bullied, informers tarred and feathered. As a result, the Royal Governor Bernard had called in the King's forces for protection. The Wheatleys along with the rest of Boston watched as three of the King's crack regiments from Halifax landed at Long Wharf along with a train of artillery. The Governor and his supporters looked smug as the troops marched up King Street, priding themselves on Boston's being put in her place like any naughty child.

But it was not that simple. With characteristic obstinancy, the people also defied the Quartering Act by refusing to shelter the troops, the majority setting out to make life miserable for anyone wearing a uniform.

Anxious to keep peace, the Governor turned Faneuil Hall and the Common over to the troops, imploring officers to keep their men in line with stern discipline. Soon every empty loft, warehouse, and storeroom bulged with soldiers. To all outward appearances people were accepting the presence of the troops, but an ominous undercurrent of resentment prompted many to say, "Sooner or later it's going to boil over. There'll be bloodshed."

The soldiers did try to get along, but it was only natural for tempers to flare when they were harangued by small boys, jostled off bridges into the water, and egged into a fight whenever they set foot in a tavern. Public opinion against him, Governor Bernard soon found himself powerless to accomplish anything. In the summer of '69 he was called to London, which pleased him as much as it did the people of Boston. Bells pealed joyously as his ship departed for England, and Thomas Hutchinson assumed the powers of Acting Governor, pending his official appointment.

But anyone expecting a change was disappointed, for Hutchinson had inherited his predecessor's problems. Tension still permeated the city, setting the stage for what happened the first Friday in March. By sundown, there were few who had not heard what had transpired down at Gray's Ropewalk during the noon hour.

It was still being discussed when several ladies gathered at the Wheatley home for a meeting of the Daughters of Liberty, a group which met regularly to spin and sew for the less fortunate. The parlor was nearly full of ladies at work when Phillis opened the door to admit Hester Beach, who had earned her reputation as a town gossip.

The continuous buzz and occasional click of the spinning wheel mingled with the rise and fall of the wool wheel to create a peculiar rhythm as Phillis sat down and began her appointed task of winding the carded wool into fleecy rolls.

"Absolutely disgraceful," Hester said as she seated herself in the cane rocker by the fireplace.

Several of the women sighed, but she was obviously not to

be diverted. She pursed her thin lips as she began knitting at a furious pace.

"I wish I knew what really happened Friday," Mary said. "I've heard only snatches. Father says it is not for women's ears."

Before Susannah could change the subject, Hester began, "Well, of course I got this second hand, but soldiers were down at the docks trying to find work."

Several ladies looked annoyed. It was a sore point that much of the work their men could do was being taken by the King's men who, already housed and fed, could afford to work for low wages.

"And one of them insulted Sam Gray," Hester continued. "Now you all know, *nobody* insults Sam Gray."

Several nodded.

"Well, it seems Sam was eating his lunch, and when the soldier asked if there was any work, Sam told him just what kind of work he'd like to see him do." The raised eyebrows and the tone of Hester's voice removed the necessity for more explicit words.

Several stopped work, needles in mid-air. "Then what happened?"

Susannah looked distraught. She motioned Phillis to bring in the refreshments. Thankful for the break, Phillis was just bringing in the tray when they heard dogs bark, then shouts. The fire bell clanged slowly at first, then loud and wild without a pause.

"That's old Brick's bell," Hannah exclaimed.

"Let us read our motto together," Susannah said. In unison they repeated the lines from Exodus, "And all the women that were wise-hearted did spin with their hands."

The shouts, the sound of running feet came from right outside the window this time. A mob. And it was coming toward the house.

The color drained from Susannah's face. Phillis felt herself tense. Both Master John and Nat were out tonight.

Suddenly the door burst open to admit Nat and a friend, Elisha Hutchinson, Hannah's nephew and son of the Governor. "Nat, your face," Phillis cried, forgetting she was among those who might consider her speaking out an affront. Nat's cheek was cut and bleeding, his right eye bruised and swelling rapidly.

"What is it? What's happened?" Susannah cried.

"We heard the fire bell. What's burning?" Mary asked.

"There is no fire,'" Elisha told them. "It's a mob—right out there. Aunt Hannah, Father's on his way down there now."

"He'll be all right." Hannah's voice sounded calm, but the others knew the effort she was making to hide her terror.

The noise outside died down as the young men went upstairs, but Susannah had barely managed to restore order when there were more footsteps. Motioning Phillis to stay where she was, Susannah opened the door herself. "Thank God," she breathed at sight of Master John and Hannah's husband, the Reverend Samuel Mather.

"We came as soon as we could." Master John shed his great coat and crossed to the fire to warm his hands. "Getting up King Street was no easy task. At least it's quiet out there now."

"But at what a price." Mather's eyes clouded with pain.

"What happened?" the ladies demanded. "Was anyone hurt?"

Master John took a deep breath. "Five dead, four badly wounded. I have never seen anything like it. A misunderstanding that exploded into senseless violence. If it weren't for the Governor . . ." his voice trailed off. "Hannah," he said, "your brother was magnificent."

"Tell us about it," she said.

Master John poured two bracers of rum and handed one to Mather. He took a gulp of his own, then said, "We still don't know how it started. Soldiers got into a fight with the men

down at the customs house, and someone went for reinforcements."

"Things might have been settled peaceably if that Crispus
Attucks hadn't shown up just then," said Mather. "All it takes
is one hothead."

"Nigger . . ." Phillis heard Hester whisper.

"He's no good," another woman chimed in. "Ran away
from someplace down south. My husband says the name isn't
even his. It's really Michael Johnson. Says he won't go by a
name any white man gave him."

"Just as well," Hester shot back. "Name's too good for him
anyhow."

Phillis felt as though every eye was on her. She realized she
was not a part of their world at all, but one with this man
they were attacking.

"Worst of it is," Master John broke in, "nobody knows
whether it was the soldiers giving orders or someone in the
mob reacting to the firebell." He shuddered. "Next thing we
know this Attucks was shot dead with four others. Murdered
right there in front of the mob." His hand trembled as he set
the mug down.

Phillis' stomach lurched. She saw the scene in vivid detail.
Blood staining the snow crimson, the screams of the victims
as they writhed in agony. She dropped the linen she was fold-
ing and ran to the shelter of her room. Why must there be
so much in the world that was ugly?

By the following day, everyone knew how courageous
Governor Hutchinson had been in disbursing the mob the
night before.

"There's no telling what might have happened if it hadn't
been for him," Mary told her parents the next day. "Reverend
John told me Hutchinson went through the heart of that mob
while they were still calling out for blood. Walked right
through them just as calm and cool and out onto the balcony
of the State House. He says the mob was ready to tear him to

pieces, but he acted like it was nothing at all."

"What happened to the soldiers who fired the guns?" Susannah asked.

"They've got them in the jailhouse," Nat said. "They're to be charged with murder today. There's a mass meeting set at Fanueil Hall at ten this morning. I hear Sam Adams is ready to settle this thing once and for all. He says every soldier is going to be routed out of Boston or else."

"I suppose you and Nat will attend the meeting?" Susannah said to her husband.

"I wouldn't miss it," he said.

Late that afternoon, the two men returned jubilant. So many people had crowded into Fanueil, the meeting had been moved to Old South Meeting House.

"And it still wasn't big enough," Nat told them. "There must have been a thousand people. They stood outside in the snow for hours waiting for the committee to get back from the State House." His eyes snapped with excitement. "I wish I could have been there. They say Adams really laid it on the line. Claims Hutchinson said he had no authority to remove more than one regiment, but Sam wasn't taking that for an answer. Stayed right there until he got him to order both regiments to Castle Island. Sam Adams strutted like a peacock when he got back and told us what happened."

"That he did, and he had reason to. It was a real victory."

"Nat, whose side are you on?" Mary demanded. "Most of the time you sound like you side with the Governor, but just now you sounded proud of Sam Adams."

"I am, Mary, and that's the hell of it. I don't know I'm on any side. Both have made mistakes." He stirred the fire with a poker. "Thing is, I'm afraid we're a long way from the end. I just hope to God they're wrong when they say we'll eventually fight to free ourselves from England."

"Let's hope it never comes to that," Nat said. "If it happens I'd rather not be here."

CHAPTER X

ALTHOUGH THE BOSTON MASSACRE, as it came to be called, soon faded into the background, the feelings it generated had far reaching effects. It was plain that however subtle the pressures, Boston was being wooed by two groups —those loyal to the Crown and those who supported the Patriots.

But politics were relegated to second place in the Wheatley family as work began on Mary's dowry. As was the custom, the women busied themselves weaving and stitching the towels, linens, and personal items she would need in her new role as Mistress Lathrop.

Late in August, Susannah told Phillis they would have an opportunity to hear the Reverend George Whitefield, who was scheduled to speak at Christ Church the following week. "It's an experience you won't soon forget," she said. "He's been speaking in the colonies since January, and they say he's never been better. They claim even his most enthusiastic followers underestimated how many converts he could draw into the fold this time."

Phillis was curious as they walked toward Christ Church.

She was glad they had heeded Reverend John's advice to come early. Even before they reached the door they could see it was going to be filled to capacity.

She looked around with interest as they entered. Not as opulent as King's Chapel, it was nevertheless beautiful in a more austere way. The rows of white pews gleamed in the light filtering down from the candles overhead. She followed Mary and Susannah through the hinged door of a pew a third of the way down. Behind the altar was a table, flanked by a red chair on either side. Over it hung a painting of Christ. In the chair to the left, she recognized the pastor of the church, while on the right sat a portly gentleman who, she guessed, must be Whitefield. Phillis craned her neck to see the man purported to be the greatest evangelist since Christ himself as he rose and acknowledged his introduction with a modest bow.

He was moderately tall, his florid face puffy. An extra chin bulged over his collar. His shoulder length wig was simple, rolled under in a small pouf. He was dressed in a black robe, a bib-like affair of white at the neck, plain white cuffs under his flowing sleeves. His mouth was pleasant with upturned lines, suggesting a man who could mix humor with his piety. He was, she decided, an ordinary looking man, with the exception of his eyes. There was a pronounced squint in one of them. The effect was a curious unmatched look.

She watched him make his way across the altar, descend into the outer aisle, then climb the winding steps into the pulpit suspended overhead. Every eye was on him as he lifted his slender hands high into the air, his delicate pointed fingers outstretched. "Praise be unto the Lord," he exulted.

The voice did not fit the man. It was rich and resonant with a musical quality which seemed to transform him into something far beyond a mere mortal.

"Brothers and sisters, I rejoice that you have come here to take that important step toward redemption along the golden pathway to eternity." He glanced at his sermon paper. "The time is fulfilled, and the kingdom of God is at hand, repent ye and believe the gospel."

His bell-like voice rose and fell dramatically, his gestures graceful and appropriate.

Phillis sat spellbound, certain he was speaking directly to her.

"How many of you think you are prepared to enter the kingdom of heaven?" he thundered. There was a ripple of response through the audience. He paused, clasping his hands behind his back to let the question sink into their minds. Then, drawing himself up to his full height, he said, "Brothers and sisters, you are badly mistaken if you think you are ready. I venture to say that *not one* of you *here* is prepared for judgment day."

He was sweating now, gesturing so wildly he knocked loose the woven tapestry cloth over the edge of the pulpit.

"Who among you has never frolicked on the Sabbath?" he roared, pointing a bony finger at them.

"Who amongst you has not danced to music played by wastrels for the purpose of luring you into the paths of Satan? And lastly, who amongst you sitting in this House of the Lord has never adorned yourself in finery so that others will take heed of what you wear?"

Phillis glanced at Mary. Dancing and pretty clothes were her greatest pleasures. Did that make her a sinner?

Whitefield stamped his feet and pounded his fist into the pulpit. His voice slashed out into the congregation like a righteous sword.

"These, brothers and sisters, are sins. We are all sinners, and unless we repent this day, we shall all perish in the pit of the damned, where the flames will burn throughout eternity."

He stopped, put a hand to one ear, and said, "Hark, hark, do you not hear him? Jehovah is pleading with you to come to this altar, be forgiven of your sins through the precious blood of our Savior, Jesus Christ."

A baby wailed, and the mother, failing to quiet him, walked rapidly toward the back of the church.

"I plead with you to throw yourselves on the mercy of our Lord, for unless you do, the devil is waiting outside this very door to snatch you into the jaws of the eternally damned. Come, come now to be saved."

Phillis thrilled to such passion. There was strength, gentleness, and pathos as he beseeched, implored, chastized them.

Again he entreated them to come forward.

No one moved.

Phillis held her breath, afraid even that slight sound would disturb the reverence of the moment.

There was a startled expression on Whitefield's face. He appeared to be listening. "Hark, what is that? Ah, the attendant angel is about to leave the threshold of the sanctuary and ascend to heaven."

He looked at them imploringly. "And shall he ascend and not bear with him the news of ONE SINNER in all this multitude reclaimed from the error of his ways?"

He looked down at them, and Phillis saw tears glisten in his eyes.

"Sinners," he cajoled in a soft voice, "who among you will be the one Gabriel shall report to God as the first to come forward?"

A black man rose and slowly shuffled down the aisle.

There was a buzz through the congregation. "It's Jeddediah Parker's man, Adam," she heard someone whisper.

"Hallelujah," Whitefield cried, his voice ringing with joy. He wiped his damp brow with a large white handkerchief. "Let us rejoice with this sinner."

Pandemonium broke loose as he stepped down from the pulpit to greet the pilgrim. People rushed headlong into the aisles, weeping and wailing, confessing their sins as though they couldn't wait to get to the altar to do it. Several fell prostrate on the floor. Immediately a group of men, who apparently traveled with Whitefield, went to rescue them. Phillis could hear them comfort those who had broken down under their burden of guilt.

She, Susannah, and Mary were carried forward by the momentum of the crowd. They could see Whitefield at the head of the aisle laying a hand on a bowed head, offering a prayer, clasping a hand. He seemed to Phillis a personification of the Holy Spirit. She trembled as they drew close.

"Dear Child." He took her hand into his sweaty ones. His luminous blue eyes looked directly into hers.

Warmth flowed through her, as though he had somehow transferred a portion of his majestic strength to her. Awed, she bowed her head, certain she would never be the same again.

"I pray you will always remember to live only for the glory of God." He released her hand.

"Now I know why you wanted me to hear him," Phillis said when the three were outside. "I felt God Himself was speaking to us through him."

"Reverend John says it's an act. He told me he's heard Whitefield practices his gestures and sermons over and over just like a stage actor," Mary said.

"Mary, don't be disrespectful of your elders," Susannah reproved.

News of Whitefield's death a few weeks later stunned Boston. The State House was promptly draped in black, bells tolled, flags flew at half mast, and ships' guns fired mourning blasts.

Phillis was surprised to realize what an impact the evangelist had made on her. She found herself thinking about him at odd moments.

"You just the same as you always was. Can't keep your mind on nothin'." Sukey complained as she hobbled around the table Phillis was wiping clean. The old cook was getting along in years, unable to do much of the actual work anymore. Master John had recently hired a woman, Mrs. Birdwell, to help with the heavy work, but Sukey still allowed no one to usurp her authority in the kitchen. Despite dim eyesight and a weak back, her tongue was as sharp as ever, and she still upbraided the others whenever she felt it necessary.

Phillis flushed at being caught daydreaming about Whitefield's sermon at Christ Church. Snatches of verse ran through her mind as she tidied the kitchen. As soon as she had finished, she found paper and quill and began to write.

> Hail happy Saint on thine immortal throne
> Possest of glory, life, and bliss unknown
> We hear no more the music of thy tongue
> Thy wonted auditories cease to throng
> Thy sermons in unequall'd accents flow'd,
> Thou didst in strains of eloquence refin'd
> Inflame the heart and captivate the mind
> Unhappy we the setting sun deplore
> So glorious once, but ah it shines no more.
> Great Countess, we Americans revere
> Thy name, and mingle in thy grief sincere.

She read it over, then folded and tucked it beneath her apron. She would send it to Whitefield's patroness, the Countess of Huntingdon in England. She wanted to do something to ease the woman's sorrow, for if she herself could feel such pain at his passing, how much more difficult for his friends so far away.

"Should I send it to her?" she asked Mary that evening.

"It's a lovely idea, Phillis," Mary smiled. "I trust this one won't bring the same consequences as the first poem you mailed to London."

"I think not," Phillis laughingly replied.

CHAPTER XI

PLANS WERE· already underway for Mary and
Reverend John's wedding at the end of January. Everyone in
the household would have a new suit of clothes, and there
must be enough food laid away, for Reverend John's family
would be coming from Connecticut.

The past months had been happy ones for Phillis. At six-
teen, she was acquiring a self-confidence never hers until now.
She spent most of her time writing, thrilled that Governor
Hutchinson himself had inquired about her progress, and that
Mr. Occom had stopped to visit while passing through Boston.

She was also becoming better acquainted with Mary's Reverend John. He frequently loaned her books belonging to the
more prominent members of his church.

His encouragement provided the motivation to complete
work on her current project, a translation of Ovid. She had
told no one, for she felt that people would only laugh at her
for attempting such an ambitious undertaking.

It was far from easy, and there were many times when she
wished she had never started, throwing down her quill and
vowing she would never finish it. But the next day would find

her pouring over the Latin text, determined to finish putting it into her own adopted tongue.

She had been so busy with it she did not even hear Nat open the library door one afternoon. Suddenly realizing he was at her shoulder startled her. She jumped, shielding the paper with one arm as she did so. "You frightened me, Mr. Nat. I didn't even hear you come in." She glanced at the clock and began gathering up her papers. "I'll leave."

"No need to stop, Phillis. I just came to get a book. Are you writing another poem?"

"Not exactly."

"What then?"

She covered the paper with her hand.

But her secrecy only seemed to intrigue him. He reached for the paper but she snatched it up.

"Promise you won't tell anyone?"

He grinned. "Cross my heart." His expression turned to utter astonishment as he read.

When he finished he looked down at her and said, "I think this should be published so others can read it."

She giggled. "Mr. Nat, even if I knew anyone who'd print it, who would ever read anything written by a slave. I do wish more people could though," she said wistfully.

"May I borrow this and your other poetry?" he asked abruptly.

"Yes, you may have it. I don't understand why, but—," she said.

"Thank you." He folded it neatly, put it in his pocket, and was gone.

She was in the pantry several weeks later counting the hams and turkeys hanging on the rafters to dry, making sure the supply of pumpkins, squash, and corn were adequate for the winter months when she heard the door open. It was Nat, looking extremely pleased.

"I have something to show you," he said, waving a paper

under her nose. "I must confess I broke my promise, Phillis. I did show your poetry to some people."

"Let me have it back, please," she said.

"I can't give it back—at least not now," he said, then smiled. "But you may have this instead."

She read with disbelief the paper he handed her. "But this is an agreement to publish. Where did you get it?"

"Didn't I tell you it was too good to keep to yourself?"

"But I don't understand . . ."

"Mr. Lathrop should get most of the credit," Nat told her. "He's the one who contacted a printer. Phillis, you're a celebrity. Everyone will soon be able to read what you've written."

She felt the warm tears on her cheeks. "Does Miss Susannah know?"

"Yes. I told her yesterday I had everything but the signature on it. Phillis, you aren't angry with me for doing this?"

She shook her head. "How could I be? It's just that I can't believe it's true."

"It is. Come, let's go upstairs and show Mother."

Surely, she thought, I'm getting all my celestial rewards right now. But deep inside she wondered. Would this be something else to alienate her from other slaves?

Outside, only the peculiar whistle summoning members to a Sons of Liberty meeting broke the silence.

CHAPTER XII

1771

A BROADSIDE of Phillis' poetry was published in late October of 1770, and in the next four months, reprinted once in Newport, four more times in Boston, once in New York and once in Philadelphia. It was received with overwhelming enthusiasm. Susannah was beside herself with pride. Only Master John suspected that in Phillis she was seeing the recognition denied her not once but twice. For his part he couldn't help feeling proud, finally admitting to himself how fond he had become of Phillis. But he was puzzled. It was a strange world where a mere slave could outshine one's own flesh and blood.

There was little time for Phillis to savor her new status, for every corner of the house would have to shine for the Wheatley wedding. Servants and family alike joined together to polish, clean, sew, and bake, none more vigorously than Phillis.

Silver gleamed and wood glowed in the flickering candlelight, as Mary became Mistress Lathrop. At that moment, Phillis would have gladly exchanged every ounce of her intellectual gifts for the privilege of being loved; for experiencing the reverence in the couple's eyes as they exchanged their vows.

The wedding over, she and Susannah were plunged head-long into the social whirl. Now that Phillis' talents were known to the entire town, she was deluged with requests to write poems commemorating births, deaths, and weddings. "Do come to tea next Tuesday afternoon and bring Phillis to read." Susannah was pleased, but never to the point of being as ecstatic as when she received an invitation to the home of Colonel Fitch. The Fitches were at the very pinnacle of Boston society.

Phillis promised to memorize every detail of the visit for Sukey and Dora. She felt guilty about being able to do things they could not share in. To compensate, she always brought home some delicacy from the tea table. What pleased them even more were the descriptive accounts Phillis gave them regarding who had attended, what each guest wore, and what was served.

Phillis was at a loss to account for the uneasiness she felt when they arrived at the Fitch mansion, for the houseman greeted them warmly, ushering them into the most sumptuous parlor she had ever seen.

"Susannah, how nice of you to come. And Phillis." Mrs. Fitch took her by the hand and led her to a cluster of guests, and announced. "This is the Wheatley's Phillis. She's come to read."

Struggling to hide her nervousness she began the reading. The nervousness vanished as she warmed to the attentive audience, completely relaxed she finished the poem written for the occasion, and began reciting from memory in response to repeated requests for "just one more, please?"

The guests crowded around her afterward. However her mind was more on food than conversation; for as usual, she had been too excited to eat beforehand. She glanced wistfully at the tea table where maids were bringing in delicate cakes, sweetmeats, elaborate flans in elegant silver bowls, and chafing dishes. Phillis began to enjoy herself immensely as she was drawn into a lively discussion of The Tenth Muse, Anne Bradstreet's book of poetry. She was listening attentively, when out of the corner of her eye she saw three young women enter the room. Were these the Fitch girls Dora always referred to as "the snobs"?

"Phillis, dear," Mrs. Fitch called. "Come meet my daughters."

Reluctantly, Phillis left the group and went to where the trio stood. Two of the three were of medium height and plump, the third tall and angular with a beak-like nose. All were dressed in elaborate gowns lavishly embroidered with the pan hoops drawn back to reveal brilliantly colored petticoats, and matching satin slippers underneath. Despite their differences, there was an uncanny sameness about them.

"I wish you girls could have been here to hear Phillis read her poems," Mrs. Fitch said. "She was delightful. Phillis, this is my Sarah, Abigail, and Flora."

"I am honored," Phillis murmured.

A servant announced tea was ready. Phillis turned and started toward the others, then stopped. Something was wrong.

Flora and her mother were speaking in low tones. Mrs. Fitch shook her head, then placed a finger to her lips and glanced at Phillis. The color rose in her face.

"Not at our table," Phillis heard Flora say. "She's a nigger ..."

"Flora ..." Mrs. Fitch's strained voice carried across the room.

"I shall *never* sit at the table with a slave." There was an audible gasp as Flora swept past the startled guests.

Sarah and Abigail remained where they were. There was no sound.

At the doorway Flora paused. "Sarah? Abigail?"

The two looked at Flora, then their mother, then slowly, heads bowed, they followed their sister.

Cheeks flaming, Mrs. Fitch made her way to the head of the table and drew herself up to her full height. "I apologize for the incident you have just witnessed, and I want you all to know neither the colonel nor myself condone our daughters' behavior." She had suddenly assumed an authority Phillis would not have dreamed her capable of just minutes before.

"Phillis?" Mrs. Fitch's voice was firm. "Will you please lead the way to the table?"

Tears burned Phillis' eyes as she filled her plate, then looked for some means of escape. She could not stay much longer without breaking down. Seeming to sense her plight, the houseman nodded toward a door at the back of the room. As soon as she felt herself unobserved, she set her plate down and fled to the kitchen, thankful to see an outside entrance.

It was there Susannah found her.

"Oh, my dear," she said. "If only I could have spared you this." She handed Phillis a fresh handkerchief. "May God have mercy on them." She sighed. "Mrs. Fitch feels terrible about this. She wouldn't have hurt you for the world." She took Phillis' hand. "Come, Prince is here to take us home."

All the way home Sukey's words, uttered so long ago, echoed in Phillis' ears. 'Trouble is, child, you don't really fit nowhere.'

CHAPTER XIII

ALTHOUGH THE EXPERIENCE at the Fitch's hurt Phillis deeply, an outpouring of invitations reassured her she was welcome in all but a few homes. But Susannah became far more selective, doing her best to not merely indulge her vanity when accepting.

Phillis' feeling of acceptance was complete on being invited to become a full member of Old South Church, a privilege rarely accorded a slave.

"Welcome to our family, Sister Phillis," the pastor, Dr. Sewell, said afterward as he clasped her hand. "I know you will be a credit to our church and your people."

"Thank you. I shall try," she said softly.

Autumn lingered that year. Mary was radiant in her new role as Mistress Lathrop, happily making plans for the baby expected the first of the year. Almost without realizing it, Phillis began to assume much of the role Mary had vacated with marriage, as she and Susannah spent many hours together in quiet companionship.

But as the weather turned brisk one cold after another plagued Phillis. Her face grew too thin, her clothes hung loosely on her, and her frequent coughing spasms became violent as they had been when she first arrived in Boston.

She spent much of her time in bed, huddled beneath the quilts, a flannel cloth around her chest to ward off drafts. Day by day the hollows in her cheeks grew deeper, her weariness more noticeable. Perhaps she could go to the country for a change of climate, the family decided, but when she was approached about it, she looked so upset the matter was dropped.

But as the year neared its end, their concern was also for Sukey. Now in her seventies, nearly blind, she could no longer leave her quarters. Each afternoon Phillis made her way, bible in hand, to the small room out back where Sukey lay, so weak she could scarcely lift her head.

"Phillis, you were sent by the Lord himself," Sukey whispered one day as Phillis finished reading the scriptures. Her stiff hand reached for Phillis', gripping it with what meager strength remained. The fatal gurgling sound far back in the old woman's throat frightened Phillis. "I'm happy to do it for you, Sukey. You rest now. I'll be back," she promised, fighting to hold back the tears.

"Don't you worry about me, child. I got everything I need right here. It's you I worry about. We're treated good here, but someday Miss Susannah an' Master John gonna die. Then you'll have to learn to fight like the rest of us." The effort to talk drained Sukey of what little strength was left. She was already dozing when Phillis tiptoed out of the room.

No words were necessary when Phillis came downstairs the next morning. One look at Susannah's strained white face, and she knew Sukey was gone.

Dora was near hysteria as she lit candles and offered frantic prayers for Sukey's soul.

Phillis, her grief like a heavy weight suspended inside her, relived the times over the years she had gone to Sukey for comfort. Never again would she feel the warmth of that ample bosom, nor the strong arms shielding her from harsh reality.

The burial was early in the morning. Needles of sleet stung their faces as the small group of family and friends made their way over the frozen ground to the grave Prince had dug the night before at the back of the lot. No matter that women seldom attended funerals during the winter months, Susannah was there, bundled in a bulky black cloak. She and Phillis huddled together drawing what little warmth they could from each other, physically and emotionally.

Prince stood apart from them, shoulders hunched, his gray head bowed. Dora's chest heaved with silent sobs. Nat and Master John stood soldier-straight, black bands around their arms and hats. Only Mary was absent, for her confinement was at hand.

They were silent as Reverend John stepped forward, prayer book open. "Let us bow our heads and pray," he said.

Phillis kept her eyes down, unable to allow herself to look at the monstrous, black draped coffin. Her mind wandered. Reverend John's words crowded out the lines of a poem she had written:

> While deep you mourn beneath the cypress shade
> The hand of death, and your daughter laid
> In dust, whose absence gives your tears to flow
> And racks your bosom with incessant woe.
> Let recollection take a tender part
> Assuage the raging torture of your heart
> Still the wild tempest of tumultous grief
> And pour the heavenly nectar of relief.

"In the name of the Father and the Son and the Holy Ghost." Reverend John closed the book.

CHAPTER XIV

MARY'S BABY, christened John Lathrop, Jr., was born a few weeks later.

"He's the most beautiful baby I ever saw," Phillis said as she gazed down at the squirming bundle in its mother's arms, and she threw herself into helping care for him.

Three weeks later, Phillis suffered a debilitating fever. This time the family knew something had to be done.

She became pale and listless. A cough chipped relentlessly at her strength, and she lost weight. "I believe she should have a doctor," she overheard Master John say to Susannah.

A doctor. The thought sent icy chills down her back. Doctors did terrible things to you and then you died anyway. According to Dora, nobody called a doctor unless they were already dying.

Dr. Richards was a kindly man with watery blue eyes nearly hidden by the enormous bags which sagged beneath them. His head reminded Phillis of a snowdrift. He listened to her chest, asked about her eating and sleeping habits, and prescribed powders for her to take twice daily.

The powders only seemed to bring on more coughing, and

over the next few weeks she submitted to all kinds of treatments. She was purged with an evil tasting liquid which left her shaken and too weak to lift her head off the pillow for three days. After that, her skin was blistered with hot mustard packs to rout out the poisons in her system; and finally, when nothing else had worked, Dr. Richards recommended blood letting.

Phillis' mouth went dry. She gritted her teeth, vowing to submit to anything if it meant she could remain in Boston. Her feeling of horror grew as the doctor reached into his bag and pulled out a fleam, a shiny instrument that gleamed where the light struck it.

"Be brave, dear," Susannah said, taking Phillis' hand. "You'll scarcely feel it."

"Just a little prick," Dr. Richards said as he picked up the fleam. "The basin, please." He took it from Mrs. Birdwell and placed it under Phillis' arm.

She gasped as it punctured her vein, biting her lip so hard she could taste blood. She had meant to keep her eyes tightly shut, but curiosity won. She opened them just in time to see dark blood drip slowly into the basin. She was suddenly light-headed. For an instant, everything in her line of vision moved helter-skelter before she was sucked down into darkness.

When she awoke, the doctor was gone. Her arm was wrapped with a clean piece of white muslin. A small glass of spirits stood on the table beside her.

Through sheer determination, and the fear of leaving the Wheatley home, Phillis improved enough in the next few weeks to be up and about a good part of the day. Her routine once again became much the same as it had been before her illness. She wrote verse, helped Susannah, and accepted what invitations her health would permit.

Two letters from England arrived on the same day in early spring. One was addressed to Nat from a Captain Calif, the other was in a feminine looking script with the letters SH intricately worked in wax. Phillis handed them to Susannah, then busied herself straightening up the room.

"Phillis, the Lord has answered my prayers. You have been invited to London to visit the Countess of Huntingdon."

"The Countess of Huntingdon? I don't understand."

"Remember when Mr. Occom was there and wrote about her being a close friend of Lord Dartmouth and George Whitefield?"

"Vaguely," Phillis answered. It made no sense. Why should such an important person be writing to Susannah?

"Apparently she was quite taken with you. Here, read the letter." Susannah handed it to Phillis.

> "My dear Mrs. Wheatley,"
> "I have made inquiries about this amazing servant girl of yours ever since receiving a copy of her poem about my dear deceased friend, Mr. George Whitefield. I have plied Mr. Occom with questions and what he has told me has only aroused my curiosity and reaffirmed my feeling I must meet her myself. It would please me if it could be arranged for her to visit me soon. I feel certain my friends at court would be delighted to meet such a talented young lady. I also understand she is not in the best of health. Perhaps we could arrange for her to see my personal physician, the honorable Dr. Fothergill."

For one luxurious moment, Phillis allowed herself to imagine what it would be like in the fairytale world of the royal court.

She handed the letter back reluctantly. The thick creamy paper, with its graceful scrolled writing, seemed a link between her life and the magic she could never know. "I'll never be able to go, but I shall always treasure the memory of having been invited," she said.

"Don't be so sure you can't go. There may be a way," Susannah said quietly.

Susannah fingered the other unopened letter. "Nathaniel is planning a trip to London to look over new merchandise."

She was silent a moment, then said, "Of course, I could never permit you to make such a trip alone, but if Nathaniel goes . . ."

Phillis' imagination soared like a seagull. A trip to England? The home of her poetic idols? She envisioned visiting the great cathedrals, perhaps even the place which had inspired Gray to write his famous elegy. Then reality crowded out the dreams.

Susannah opened the top drawer of her dresser and took out a pack of letters tied with a pink ribbon. She added the letter to the packet, retied the ribbon, and replaced them in the drawer. "Let's not mention this to anyone for the present," she whispered to the astonished Phillis.

CHAPTER XV

1773

"SUSANNAH, have you gone mad? Of course Phillis can't go to London. I will hear no more on the matter."

"But the doctor says she must have a change of climate if she is to survive. And Nat will watch over her. It's not as though she were going off alone."

"Do you think for one minute I will tolerate a slave purchased on the marketplace to be feted by nobility? To be given a place higher than my own wife? My own children? Spare me further arguments."

Susannah retreated, but only for the moment. Having Phillis make the journey was next to going herself. She had handled John before. She would do it now.

It had all started so casually. Even when the Countess had first mentioned the possibility of having Phillis come, Susannah had merely thought it a courteous gesture of gratitude for Phillis' having written the poem about Whitefield.

In the end, it was Reverend John who broke down his father-in-law's resistance, and convinced him Phillis should go. Over and above the question of her health, he said, "Meeting the Countess is an opportunity for spiritual enrichment she may never know otherwise. I cannot help but feel Phillis has been marked for some kind of divine mission in this life. Are we to thwart what may be God's will?"

Master John sighed. "I strongly suspect my wife and daughter have gotten to you first, but I admit you have given me reason to reassess my opinion." He paused. "So long as she is with Nathaniel, she may go."

Never had Phillis felt more like throwing her arms around him and kissing him, but "Thank you, Master John," was all she said. "And you too, Reverend John."

Susannah threw herself into a frenzy of preparation for Phillis' proper presentation and attire. Mary too, had insisted on outfitting Phillis in lovely gowns of mauve, blue, and grey silks, selected from the finest bolts of fabrics from her father's shop.

"She won't be a servant there. No white apron and cap. She is going as a guest," Mary had argued.

Nobody, not even Phillis herself, sensed the turmoil inside Susannah as the day of departure drew close. *Why, I love her every bit as much as I do Mary*, she realized with a sense of wonder. *She's my daughter as surely as though I had nurtured her in my own womb.*

Phillis waved one last time to the family assembled on the wharf as the boat edged away from shore, excitement intermingled with sadness at leaving loved ones. How had she failed to notice that pinched look to her mistress' features these past weeks? The many times she had stopped in the midst of a task to rest for a moment?

"I'm worried about your mother," she said abruptly to Nat. "She's not looking well."

"Phillis, this is supposed to be a holiday for you. The last thing you're to do is fret about anything." He smiled. "Think of the good times you shall have once we arrive. I have a feeling you are going to enchant all of London. You are very pretty, you know."

She felt herself flush at the unexpected compliment. Boston was only minutes behind them, but already she felt their relationship had altered in a subtle way she did not understand. Was this a taste of the freedom that Obour had spoken of with such passion?

The outline of the State House dominated the skyline, its flag fluttering gently in the breeze. How long would it be before she saw it again?

Later that night she wrote:

> Adieu New England's smiling meads
> Adieu, the flowery plain;
> I leave thine opening charms, O spring,
> And tempt the roaring main.
>
> In vain for me the flow-rets rise
> And boast their gaudy pride
> While here beneath the Northern skies
> I mourn for health deny'd.
>
> Celestial maid of rosy hue
> O let me feel thy reign!
> I languish til thy face I view
> Thy vanish'd joys regain.

Susannah mourns, nor can I bear
To see the crystal shower.
Or mark the tender falling tear
At sad departure's hour;

Not unregarding can I see
Her soul with grief oppressed
But let no sigh, nor groans for me
Steal from her gentle breast.

In vain the feather'd warblers sing
In vain the garden blooms
And on the bosom of the spring
Breathes out her sweet perfumes.

While for Brittania's distant shore
We sweep the liquid plain
And with astonished eyes explore
The wide-extended main.

She had written twelve stanzas. She would send it to her
mistress as soon as she could. Now she must think ahead.

CHAPTER XVI

THEY WERE ON THE SEAS for nearly two months.
Some days, propelled by a favorable wind, they made good
time, on others they barely moved; but except for a brief

bout with rough seas which made Phillis wish she had never left Boston, it was a pleasant voyage.

And then, there it was at last. England, its splendorous vivid green shore enhanced by the majestic chalk white cliffs in the background.

Her excitement mounted as they drew closer, finally gliding between the two immense rocks which guarded the inner harbor at Portsmouth. Now she could clearly make out the dirty smokestacks, the dingy warehouse buildings, and the wharves reaching out into the water like huge fingers.

She peered at the brick walls of what looked to be an ancient cathedral. She felt magically swept back in time, could almost imagine she heard the shouts of Roman conquerors.

They were on their way to London by stage long before sunrise the next day along with two other passengers. A cantankerous old man dozed in one corner, his face grooved with scowl lines. The other, a nattily dressed gentleman, offered Phillis a pillow to make her journey more comfortable. He was also a merchant, and he and Nat were soon discussing business, leaving her to enjoy the scenery.

She had never seen anything so green. For two days they made their way through gently rolling hills, broken by thatched roofs, stone fences marking off pastureland, and cows placidly chewing clover.

Now and then they passed through a village, a cluster of cottages usually huddled around a church, rambling ivy or roses softening the austere stone walls.

Even the air smelled different as they drew closer to London, a thick pall of gray fog replacing the fine country mist. Villages were closer together now as the pace quickened and more vehicles choked the road. Paddington, Marybone, Pentenville, Euston. In each, she watched women lay out their wash to dry on bushes and tend small gardens. Several times they slowed to make way for children driving cows or pigs up the road.

Their first view of London was an endless maze of church spires and chimneys jutting into the sky like huge exclamation points. Now they were in the city itself, the horses' hoofs pounding against the cobblestones. There was a sense of the old mingling with the new, ugliness mixed wantonly with beauty. The air was heavy with the odor of soap boilers and factories, the rotten smell from the open sewage canals and refuse piled in the gutters. It amazed Phillis to find that instead of being offended by them, she felt strangely stimulated.

They were in the midst of the city now, row after row of dingy brick houses lining both sides of the street, each story overhanging the one underneath so that the alleys separating them were shut off from light. Gaudy signs swung in every block. "Children Educated Here," "Funerals Furnished Here," and the one which made them chuckle, "Ye Public House," the bold letters read, "Drunk for a Penny, Dead Drunk for a Tuppence, Clean Straw to Lie On for Nothing."

She shuddered at the thought of even entering the filthy building, let alone sleeping there.

"Not much like home, is it?" Nat remarked.

She shook her head, still absorbed in watching the vendors stroll the streets calling out their wares in sing-song voices, beggars and cripples huddled in dark doorways. She never dreamed streets could be so congested.

They crossed the Thames at Westminister Bridge, and within minutes the streets began to look cleaner. Taverns replaced tenement buildings, and large neat houses with squared off lawns made it difficult to believe they were only minutes from the slums they had just passed through.

The merchant was busy pointing out landmarks. Wren's work of art, St. Paul's Cathedral, like a beacon over the city, government buildings flanking the river, Mansion House, the Lord Mayor's home.

It was late afternoon when they pulled up in front of the station where the Countess' driver was to meet them. Panic gripped Phillis as she realized they were nearly there.

Sensing her nervousness, Nat patted her hand. "You've nothing to worry about, Phillis. Anyone who can read poetry to a roomful of Boston bluenoses can handle anything."

She wished she thought so. Phillis was happy that Nat was to stay a few days before beginning his business negotiations.

The carriage, which arrived a quarter of an hour later, was an ornate one, a coat of arms painted on the side in gilded letters. She liked the nimble driver on sight. He spoke briefly to the stationmaster, then turned to them.

"You must be the Wheatleys," he said.

Nat nodded.

"Welcome to London. McIvars the name, sir. Thomas McIvars. Lady 'untingdon's coachman." His pale blue eyes were merry under his cap from under which stuck out a hatch of straw colored hair. "Worked for the Countess near fifteen year, I 'ave." He gave Phillis an appraising glance and broke into a grin. "You must be the one 'er ladyship is so taken with. Blimey, she's talked of nothing but you for weeks now."

Phillis warmed to his obvious approval. She felt as though she had passed the first hurdle.

McIvars saw them into the carriage, then hoisted their luggage onto the rack and climbed into the driver's seat. Phillis was curious about him. "Is he a slave?" she asked Nat.

"No. England outlawed slavery three years ago. Everyone who works here is paid wages."

Wages? No slavery? The thought that she was actually in a country where no one could buy or sell a person staggered her. And if the colonies belonged to England, and Parliament made the laws, why was there slavery in one part of the empire and not in another? There was much she did not understand.

McIvars gave the horses a smart slap on the flank as they turned off Euston Road. Another turn and they came to a gatehouse on the right. At a wave from McIvars, the huge iron gates swung open to let them through, then clanged shut behind them.

The narrow road was flanked on both sides by huge trees that looked like they had been there for centuries. Branches intermingled overhead so that only a little light flickered through to make a faint lacy pattern on the road ahead. Then, so abruptly Phillis was startled, they rounded a wide curve to see ahead of them, surrounded by a wide expanse of green lawn, the biggest house Phillis had ever seen.

There was an incredible sense of order in the gently sloped terrace and formal gardens beyond. McIvars guided the horses up the drive and stopped directly in front of the entrance, on either side of which crouched a huge stone lion. To their right, a fountain sent spray into the air in a graceful arc. It's not real, Phillis thought. Any moment she was going to open her eyes and find herself back on King Street.

"Step carefully," McIvars warned as they alighted. Phillis looked out over the trim lawn then back to the carved marble columns lining the veranda on either side, feeling as she had that day so long ago when she and Susannah had stood outside the Tanner house.

Nat held her arm. Her knees shook as the huge doors opened.

"My dear Phillis—and Mr. Wheatley. I am Lady Huntingdon. Welcome to London, and Huntingdon House."

CHAPTER XVII

A CONFUSION of contradictory thoughts swept over Phillis as they stepped into the marble entry hall. The warmth of Lady Huntingdon's greeting dispelled much of her fear, but she was conscious of a sharp feeling of disappointment. Never had she pictured a lady of nobility as being other than tall and regal, dressed in elaborate gowns, her throat adorned with priceless jewels, hair piled fashionably on her head.

Instead, the buxom woman before them was shorter than she. She wore sombre gray muslin, its drabness accentuated by the mud-colored woolen shawl around her shoulders, and no jewelry. Only the high ruched cap of white muslin tied under her ample chin, relieved the severity of her costume. Nat, too, was obviously trying hard to conceal his surprise.

"I trust your trip has not been too unpleasant," the woman said. "I am so anxious to get acquainted, but I know you must be tired and would welcome the chance to rest and refresh yourselves first."

She led the way through the long hallway past a gallery, where Phillis glimpsed high white walls broken only by tall alabaster columns delicately veined in purple. Statues of marble and porcelain housed in niches, stared out at her like a courtroom full of judges.

As they started up the staircase, Phillis looked at the golden banisters with genuine awe. She would feel no surprise should the Gate of St. Peter appear at the top.

Upstairs, the Countess led them down the long hallway. "Your room, Mr. Wheatley." She indicated the first door on the right. Nat thanked her and stepped inside.

She continued on. "I have put you down the hall, Phillis, I hope you will like it. It was my daughter's room many years ago, and it seemed just right for you."

She opened the door and stepped back to let Phillis into the large airy room. Beside the window stood a marble-topped table on which a vase of   tear drop glass reflected the sun's rays into dazzling pinpoints of color.

On the opposite wall was a fireplace, the hearthstones set in marble, and on the remaining wall a bed nearly twice the size of the one at home. Phillis could imagine the time and effort spent polishing the carved bedposts and matching cornice to such perfection. The heavy damask bedcurtains were a delicate shade of lime green, embroidered with gold dragons, the walls hung with matching damask. Even the drapes at the windows were of the same material, drawn back and tied with thick gold tassels. Near them a small dressing table with a fresh bouquet of yellow roses and a dainty gold chaise lounge completed the furnishings.

"Here is Colette to light the fire." Lady Huntingdon said, "although I must warn you most of the heat and very little of the smoke goes up the chimney. I hope you brought something warm to wear. These rooms are always cold, even this time of year. This shawl is the only thing that keeps me warm. Of course, my daughters scold because it is not a thing of beauty. It bothers them that I do not dress more elegantly, but I tell them if the Lord had felt such fripperies necessary,

He would certainly have endowed us with them as He did the flowers in the fields and the birds in the sky."

Phillis smiled, conscious of being at ease for the first time since landing at Portsmouth. The Countess looked much younger than her sixty-five years, her face interesting rather than beautiful. Triangular shaped, it revealed a strong bone structure. The nose was too sharp, the eyes too deep set under the heavy brows for beauty, but when she smiled it was as though a candle had been lit inside her illuminating every feature.

She took hold of Phillis' hands. "You can't know how I have prayed for this chance to know you, my dear."

"I still can't believe you would ask me here when you knew nothing about me," Phillis said.

"But that is where you are wrong. I know a great deal about you. You realize, of course, it began when I received the poem you wrote in Mr. Whitefield's memory." Her eyes filled with pain.

Phillis told about her experience at Christ Church. "One does not need to know a man well to perceive greatness," she finished quietly.

Lady Huntingdon nodded. "I know. I first heard him thirty-five years ago." Her eyes took on a far away look. "I remember as though it were yesterday. When he finished I felt as though the Lord Himself had spoken to me personally." She was silent for a moment. "I content myself in furthering the work he started."

She glanced at the clock on the wall. "What am I thinking of? You're weary after that long journey. We dine downstairs at seven. You need not worry about dressing. There will be enough of that later, for everyone is clamoring to meet you. Tonight just wear what you feel comfortable in." She indicated the cord next to the bed. "Just ring for Colette if you need anything." She closed the door behind her.

What an unusual person! Phillis loosened her bodice and

slipped off her shoes. She looked out over the perfectly mani-
cured lawns. If anyone just a few months ago had predicted
her coming here, she would have laughed. She recalled a
sermon shortly before their departure. "The Lord has signalled out only a few for His divine grace." Surely, she
thought, this is proof I must be one of them. She had no
doubt God had plucked her out of that slave market to be
entrusted to the Wheatleys. But why?

She had no trouble fitting into the rhythm of Huntingdon
House. She spent the first few days exploring the house and
grounds, especially the library where, with a roaring fire to
warm her, she curled up in a high-backed velvet chair and
buried herself in one book after another.

She had a moment of misgiving when the Countess informed her she had arranged a dinner party. "Just close
friends," she said. "I thought it would be nice, since Mr.
Wheatley leaves shortly for Southampton. And I do want to
include him."

Phillis was glad. The thought of a big party made her
nervous. She needed Nat's moral support.

"Lord and Lady Dartmouth will be here, of course," the
Countess continued. "They are anxious to meet you. Lady
Catherine is a dear. I feel certain you two will get on fa-
mously."

Phillis felt a brief flash of her old insecurity as the Countess
talked about her becoming friends with a titled lady, but she
was already aware that anyone the Countess befriended was
accorded the same treatment as the most nobly born.

"But I have nothing suitable to wear until my baggage
arrives," Phillis protested.

"I think we can remedy that. It is foolish of me, I know,
but . . ." her eyes measured Phillis, "yes, you are near the
same size I once was. Long ago I had a gown made especially
to wear to the Prince of Wales' birthday party. It was so
beautiful I saved it, thinking perhaps one of my daughters

would wear it, but they took after their father in size." She sighed. "And so it has hung in the wardrobe all these years. How often I have wished it could be worn again."

Phillis was speechless when Colette appeared with the dress. The black velvet petticoat was embossed with a vase made of tiny tufts of brightly colored chenille, the flowers climbing gracefully over the full skirt. The overdress of white satin was embroidered with gold flowers, worked in tiny intricate stitches, the chenille vase and flowers motif repeated on the train.

Phillis caught her breath. How would it feel to wear a dress like this when she had never worn anything but black, with a white collar for special occasions? This was a dress for a lady of high birth. She shook her head. "I've never worn anything like this," she said.

Lady Huntingdon broke into a hearty laugh. "Then it is high time you did. The matter is settled. Colette, see that it is ready for the party."

Phillis liked the little French maid and was glad when she came to help her dress for the party. She had been with the Countess for three years, she told Phillis as she laced her bodice. "Madame says we must do something with your hair." Already Colette was brushing, twirling, pulling a ringlet out here, tucking a piece up there. She stepped back to admire the effect. "Ahh, lovely. Now for the powder." She draped a large piece of muslin over Phillis' shoulders.

"Powder? I don't think so . . ."

"Oh, but we must. All the ladies will have powdered hair. Hold still."

The clouds of powder set Phillis coughing so hard her shoulders shook.

"There," Colette said. "It makes your eyes so beautiful. Here, we put a flower on this side, so?" She picked a blossom out of the fresh bouquet on the table and secured it, then surveyed her work with a critical eye. "One more thing. A beauty patch ... here, I think. Ahh, perfect. Look in the mirror."

Phillis blinked in astonishment. The white hair did make her eyes the focal point of her face, enhancing the honeyed brown of her skin. She felt the blood rise to her cheeks as she looked down at the low cut neckline, where the top of the bodice barely covered the swelling of her firm breasts.

Nat's approval was evident as he escorted her downstairs. "Mother always said you were beautiful," he said, "but this is unbelievable."

She felt surprisingly at ease as they descended the stairs.

"Come, I want you both to meet my dear friend, Lord Dartmouth," the Countess greeted them.

He looked like a Lord, Phillis decided. Aristocratic, aloof, tall—in his late thirties or early forties she judged—the beginning of a paunch under his satin waistcoat. The pale blue eyes, the pale complexion under his meticulously styled gray wig added to his cold formality. She couldn't have been more surprised when he smiled, for it was warm and genuine, completely contradicting her first impression.

"So this is the sable muse." Taking her hand in his, he quoted from memory:

> "Should you my Lord while you pursue my song
> Wonder from wence my freedom sprung
> Wence flow these wishes for the common good
> By feeling hearts alone best understood."

She smiled. "How sweet of you to remember the words." It had to be at least two years since she had sent him the verse.

He bowed. "I am not in the habit of receiving poetry from beautiful young ladies. It was an occasion to remember."

So this was the man for whom the new Dartmouth College in New Hampshire had been named. "I have heard so much about you, your Lordship. Mr. Occom told us he never would have been able to raise sufficient funds for his school without your help."

"He is the one who convinced me it was a worthy cause," he replied. "Along with the Countess here."

Phillis liked him. She recalled hearing that of all the nobility who had flocked to the Countess' home to hear Whitefield speak, Dartmouth was the only one who had embraced the movement.

"I hope you do not intend to monopolize the guest of honor all evening, William."

Lady Catherine was younger than her husband, her features small, her nose upturned, a deep cleft in her chin, violet blue eyes slanted just enough to be arresting. Although she was no longer slim—Colette had told Phillis they were the parents of several boys—it only seemed to enhance her femininity.

She was dressed the way Phillis expected all ladies to be. Her gown was lavender brocade with purple accents. An amethyst pendant rested in the hollow of her milk white throat, and her hair was powdered and dressed in a high bouffant style which must have taken hours to create, decorated with jeweled combs and feathers. She immediately took Phillis in hand, introducing her to the other guests.

At dinner, Phillis was delighted to find herself beside Lady Catherine and opposite Nat. Beside him was Lord Dartmouth, on the other side Mr. Watson, the Lord Mayor of London; for they were seated according to tradition, ladies on one side of the table, gentlemen on the other.

She glanced down the length of the massive table as servants brought food in gleaming silver bowls. The immense chandelier overhead must have contained hundreds of candles, for the light flickering down was almost as bright as daylight, highlighting the brightly colored costumes of both men and women until it looked like a field of flowers sprinkled with jewels.

Each course was followed by another, more food than Phillis could imagine at one sitting. She was enjoying herself immensely, when she heard the Lord Mayor say between bites of poached salmon, "You don't really think, Mr. Wheatley, those farmers in the colonies will actually revolt against the Crown, do you?"

Nat flushed, but before he could answer, Lord Dartmouth broke in. "That's utter nonsense. They wouldn't dare go that far."

"No," Dartmouth continued, "they don't dare risk losing our protection. Without us France would be right back in North America, and then where would the colonies be? Besides," he went on, clearly enjoying this chance to expound on his theories. "I fear they are much like small children. If by some chance they were to become independent of us, they would be at each other's throats in a matter of weeks."

"Of course," Dartmouth continued, "they can stir up quite an uproar. I dread what might happen if any of the Hutchinson-Oliver correspondence ever gets back to the colonies."

Lord Watson's mouth twitched. "The governor *was* rather candid about the situation, wasn't he."

"It could ruin Hutchinson if it ever gets into the wrong hands," Dartmouth replied. "Personally, I can't help admire the man. He certainly can put those peasants in their place."

Phillis looked at Nat. What did he mean?

"As for your agent, Dr. Franklin," Dartmouth went on, "We'd all like to see him packed back to the colonies. He's a shrewd man, but too good a patriot. The first thing he did when I took office was badger me about that blasted petition to have the Assembly go back to paying the governor's salary. And he doesn't give up. I have a feeling whatever we say is reported word for word straight back to the radicals. Trouble is, we have no excuse to get rid of him."

The talk drifted to other subjects, but the tension lingered. Somehow the food, so delicious moments before, no longer tasted quite the same. Later in her room, Phillis pondered Nat's words over and over, vaguely acknowledging a strange sense of foreboding in them.

CHAPTER XVIII

NAT AND A MR. THORNTON left for Southampton
a few days later, and Phillis settled into a comfortable routine.
At times, she accompanied Lady Huntingdon on her pilgrimages to hospitals and into the poorer districts to distribute
food and nurse the sick. Other mornings, the Countess was
off to meetings, leaving Phillis free to browse in the library
or enjoy the gardens.

She was also feeling better. She coughed rarely now. Apparently a change of climate had been the proper prescription
for her ailments.

What intrigued her most was the contrast between Lady
Huntingdon's life and that of her friends. All deeply religious
people, their homes were alike, but they did not dress in drab
clothes, nor was the food on their tables the plain fare the
Countess favored. Their main meals consisted of seven or
eight courses, lasting several hours, followed by a late evening
repast of cold meats, jellied salads, and extravagant sweets,
ending long after the Countess had retired for the night.

Phillis loved the early afternoons when visitors would flock
to Huntingdon House to have a word with its mistress. They

were a fascinating panorama of people ranging from a minister in His Majesty's cabinet, to a poor parishioner who had
trudged miles to thank the Countess for her attentions to his
sick wife.

Phillis wondered if the Countess had always been like this
and if so, why she lived in this ornate mansion instead of a
home more suited to her spartan living habits.

Many of the answers came from Lady Hastings, for she
stopped by for tea nearly every other day. The Countess had
not always lived like this, she told Phillis. Indeed, when she
and the Earl lived in Donnington Park their dinners were the
most lavish of any in Leichestershire.

The Countess had bustled in at this point. "What are you
doing, Betty? Letting skeletons out of the closet? If so, I hope
you make it clear the best thing that ever happened to me was
becoming a Methodist."

"Was your husband a Methodist too?" Phillis asked.

"No, I was never able to convince him he should join. Not
that he wasn't a good Christian man," she hastened to add,
"but he maintained being a member of the Church of England
was enough. He felt no need to embrace Wesley's doctrines."

"Did he ever change his thinking?"

Lady Huntingdon looked serious. "No, he didn't. He never
interfered with my attending Wesley's meeting. And he extracted one promise from me which has made me debate with
my conscience more than once." She paused. "He asked me
on his deathbed to promise I would always maintain a home
suitable to the station he had achieved in life so that our
family name would continue to be respected."

So that explained the house.

"I had known religion before my husband's death, of
course," the Countess continued, "but it was only after he
was gone that I realized what a comfort it can be. Without
the task of furthering the Methodist program, I fear I should
have lost my sanity."

"What she won't tell you is how generous she was. Without her, the Methodist movement would have died for want of funds," said Lady Betty.

The Countess appeared uncomfortable. "I did what little I could."

"Stop being so modest." Lady Betty turned to Phillis. "Selina sold every jewel she owned and most of her wardrobe, and do you know what she did with the proceeds?" She bobbed her head to emphasize her words. "She bought up every old building she could find and had them repaired and painted to use as chapels. Sixty-six of them. And she bought an old castle in North Wales and set it up as a college to train clergymen."

"Where there are chapels there must be someone to preach in them," Lady Huntingdon said lightly. "Besides, what need had I for exquisite jewels and fancy clothes?" Her eyes glowed with an inner spark. "The Lord cares not what you wear, only that you live by His commandments and spread the light of His word among those in darkness."

Never had Phillis known anyone who lived God's word so completely. She wondered if she would ever have the inner discipline being a real Christian required, as she read the scriptures with a new depth of understanding.

Nat was still in Southampton when Lady Huntingdon told Phillis she would be away for several days touring her chapels.

"I dislike leaving you, dear, but Mr. Wheatley should be back any day, and of course Colette and the rest of my staff will see to your needs."

"Don't worry about me. I'll be fine," Phillis assured her.

Lady Huntingdon looked about to say something else. "I may have news for you when I return," she began, then shook her head. "I'm afraid I have a habit of speaking impulsively. Forget I said anything. You shall know when the time comes."

CHAPTER XIX

NAT RETURNED a few days later, pleased the negotiations he had come to England for had turned out far better than he had anticipated. "Both Thornton and Calif," he told Phillis, "propose I join them and manage the London office, so they can be free to oversee the ships and take care of clients in other ports." He paused. "I must say it is an attractive offer. They asked if I would remain a few months longer, at least until they complete the arrangements."

Phillis was stunned. She never dreamed his business in England would not be concluded promptly so they could return to Boston together. Surely he couldn't be seriously considering staying here. "But it's so far from home," she protested.

"I know. That's the reason I only agreed to stay on a temporary basis, and let them know my decision when I've had time to think it over."

Phillis felt reassured. She comforted herself with the thought he was too level-headed to make any rash decision. But a small doubt lingered. What was it Lady Catherine had said just the other day? "I think your Master Wheatley is quite taken with Mistress Sally Thornton," she had confided.

Now Phillis recalled that Sally, daughter of the senior partner of the firm Nat had been invited to join, was a comely young lady. So that explained Nat's dining at the Thorntons so often. She berated herself for having failed to notice.

"By the way," Nat was saying, "I heard something that may tie in with what Dartmouth was referring to at the dinner party. It concerns some letters someone got hold of that Hutchinson and Oliver wrote back a few years ago. I haven't been able to learn anything of the contents other than it's being claimed the letters prove they were both loyalists while pretending to sympathize with the colonists."

"I find it hard to believe Governor Hutchinson would do such a thing," Phillis said, remembering the compassionate man she had met so long ago. "Remember the night of the massacre when he stood up to that mob? Just think what might have happened if he hadn't stopped them when he did."

Nat nodded. "I hope no one gets hurt. Anything that throws a bad light on the governor is bound to affect our shipping business. There's no reasoning with people when they're aroused. And if Sam Adams gets wind of anything like this, he'll get people all fired up with only one side of the story."

"Maybe it's not that bad. You know how rumors are, and that's really all you've heard. There's probably some simple explanation."

"I hope you're right, but it seems to me the colonies are headed on a course to destruction. We have a few people in Parliament standing up for us, but there are a lot more who have vowed to teach us a lesson. You heard what Dartmouth said about wishing they could get rid of Benjamin Franklin."

"Is Lord Dartmouth in favor of laws that put us down?" Phillis was almost afraid to ask, for she had grown fond of him.

Nat hesitated, then said, "Dartmouth means well, I suppose, but he's not noted as being a person who gets things done. I hear that while he was most cooperative in meeting Franklin for talks, even led him to believe he would intercede on his behalf, he actually didn't lift a finger to straighten things out." He grinned rakishly. "A good many in the House of Lords call him "the one who wears a coronet and prays." They say he's better at singing psalms than making laws, and I understand it's being said the King would make him Lord of the Royal Bedchamber if the title wasn't too suggestive for his pious soul."

It was good to have Nat back. She felt flattered that he discussed national affairs with her. How their relationship had changed once they set foot on free soil.

The Countess returned, bustling into the room for breakfast the next day with a thick packet of letters in her hand. "I have a task for you," she said, "but first there is something I must confess."

Phillis smiled. "Confess?"

Lady Huntingdon's eyes twinkled as she lowered herself into a chair. "Yes. You see, dear, your trip here was not as spontaneous as you have been led to believe. You recall I told you I became interested in you while Mr. Occom was here?"

Phillis nodded.

"And that was long before I received your poem. Mr. Occom was so taken with you I was curious about your background. It was at his suggestion I began corresponding with your mistress."

Phillis was speechless. They had been corresponding all this time and Miss Susannah had never revealed it.

"I have talked with Lord Dartmouth about this," Lady Huntingdon said, "and we feel it is time to reveal the real purpose behind your visit. I have contacted a publisher here in London, a Mr. Bell, who is anxious to print a book of your poetry." She smiled. "I realize this is sudden, but we felt it best to have the preliminary arrangements completed before saying anything about it. I couldn't bear to have you disappointed if things did not work out."

"I still can't understand . . ."

"There were many people involved."

"Did Nat know about it?"

The Countess smiled. "Yes. I can tell you now that getting you here was our most perplexing problem. I was prepared to come get you myself when we learned of this business transaction between Mr. Wheatley and Captain Calif. It seemed the perfect solution. We first approached your mistress with the idea many months ago, and she was most agreeable. I wrote her at the time, saying I had talked with a printer and wanted copies of your work for him to see. We, of course, had already shown him the poem you sent me and the one to Lord Dartmouth to give him an idea of what you could do."

Susannah sent copies of her work? It was incredible. "What would you have done if there had been no way of getting me here?" Phillis asked impishly.

"We'd have thought of something." She smiled. "Come, say something. What do you think of the idea?"

"It's so overwhelming I don't know what to say."

"Incidentally, I asked your mistress to have a picture made of you to use in the front of the book. I trust it was accomplished. We thought it best to have it made in your usual surroundings to show you as you were when you wrote the poems."

"It was made a few days before I left," Phillis replied. So that was why Susannah had been so insistent about it. "She said she wanted it so she could feel I was still close by."

"No doubt she did," the Countess answered, "and so it will serve a double purpose. I have not received it yet, but I imagine it will be here soon." Her tone became businesslike. "And now I have a favor to ask."

Phillis looked up.

"I wonder, would you be able to find it in your heart to dedicate the book to me? I suppose it is vanity, but nothing would please me more than your indulging this whim of mine." She looked uncertain, as though she had spoken out of turn.

"I shall be happy to. I consider it an honor to be asked."

"I realize I am competing with your family for the honor, but I know there will be other opportunities for them." The Countess' husky voice revealed the depth of her emotion. "I feel confident this is just the beginning for you, Phillis."

"This is more than I ever hoped for."

The Countess blew her nose, then said, "Let's get to work. Mr. Bell wants the dedication within the next few days, and the sooner we take care of these details, the sooner you will hold the book in your hands. Here is paper, and there is ink there in the stand. I must see to things elsewhere."

Alone, Phillis sharpened the quill, dipped it into the inkwell, then realized she was at a loss for words. After all, she was a poet. She decided to write it as simply as she could.

She began to write slowly, gaining momentum as the words shaped themselves in her mind.

> Dedicated to the right honorouble, the Countess of Huntingdon. The following poems are most respectfully inscribed by her much obliged, very humble and devoted servant.

She read it over, then, satisfied, wrote her name, the upward strokes strong, her looped letters tall and graceful.

She felt twelve years old again and she skipped upstairs two at a time.

CHAPTER XX

"CONGRATULATIONS," Nat said to Phillis when she told him about the book, but he cut her short when she launched into the details. "You'll have to tell me all that later, I'm afraid. I've a meeting I must go to." He was out the door, leaving her puzzled. Certainly after his enthusiasm when her poetry was published three years ago, she had expected more from him than this. But he had been distracted for several days now, barely answering a greeting with a brusque nod, eating his meals in silence.

"Business problems, most likely," the Countess said. "It will pass, and he'll be his old self again."

But as the month wore on, he grew not merely distracted but irritable, and when he sent Colette from the dining room in tears because his eggs were slightly overdone, Phillis could stand it no more.

"Nat, what's the matter?" she demanded.

"Nothing," he growled.

"Yes, there is. You barely speak to anyone, not even me."

"I'm sorry, Phillis. It's this political thing, and now this letter from Mother that came yesterday."

"Politics. There are always people so hungry for power they'll destroy someone else to get it." He drummed his fingers on the table. His gray eyes blazed. "To be honest, this is one reason I'm considering that offer from Thornton. I've known for years there will be no peace in the colonies until they fight to free themselves from England, and frankly, I want no part of it."

"But, Nat, Boston's your home."

"But only as part of England. I'm just not sympathetic to what the radicals are preaching. I don't think we've been treated that badly."

"But the Stamp Act . . ."

"It was repealed, wasn't it?" he shot back. "No, Phillis, I just can't see why a compromise can't be worked out. I know that from being here, away from the vicious propaganda those radicals spread." He paused. "Did you know Massachusetts is the colony that gives the King the most trouble? They call her the "powderkeg of America" over here, full of grown men who act like children. I didn't mean to get so agitated, but I'm afraid it isn't just this Hutchinson thing I'm worked up about."

"She's not ill, is she?"

"No, nothing like that. It's just that things are bad in Boston."

"What's happened?"

"She wrote that someone from here sent letters that Governor Hutchinson and Andrew Oliver wrote during and after the Stamp Act. They were read to the legislature and printed in the paper, and now everyone believes he was conspiring with the King all along, that he was never on the colonial side, but according to my father, the letters that appeared in the paper were not the ones Hutchinson actually wrote. He says they were doctored to make it look as though he was against the people."

"But why would anyone do a thing like that?"

"You mean there's something else?"

He nodded.

"According to Calif," Nat explained, "England will retain her tax. It is bound to fire up the Colonies. Parliament has reduced the price of tea from twenty shillings to ten a pound, and has given the East India Company a monopoly to export and sell direct to the colonies in its own vessels. That way, they won't be required to stop at British ports, so they eliminate the export tax and can afford to undersell the Dutch."

At a deep sigh from Phillis, he looked contrite. "Look, I'm sorry I bothered you with all this. Here's a letter for you from Mother. I'm sure the news will be pleasanter." He handed it to her, then left.

She opened the letter and smiled at Miss Susannah's account of little Johnny's progress, and that Mary was well and looking forward to a new baby expected toward the end of the year.

There was no hint as to the state of her mistress' health. Phillis wondered how long it would be before she would see her again. In fact, more and more plans were being made as though she would be here a year from now. She must talk with the Countess soon about it.

But in the delightful days that followed, there was little opportunity for such a talk. There was a never ending round of social gatherings and picnics in the countryside. At one party, the Lord Mayor presented Phillis with a copy of Milton's *Paradise Lost*, beautifully bound in hand-tooled leather.

"Thank you, my Lord," she said. "I don't know what I've done to deserve such an honor."

"It is merely our way of showing you how much we enjoy having you among us."

She felt her loyalties being tested and knew she must make some decision soon.

CHAPTER XXI

TOWARD THE END OF AUGUST, the Countess revealed plans for Phillis to be presented to the King and Queen as soon as the Court returned from the summer residence. "Their Majesties know your book is scheduled for publication soon," she said, and they are anxious to meet you."

"But Lady Huntingdon, I'm not worthy of such an honor."

"Nonsense. If you have one fault, it is your infernal modesty. Besides, Lord Dartmouth has already set things in motion. You would have been presented before now had the royal family been at the Palace."

"I'm afraid to meet the King."

"You have no reason to be."

"But I have. Years ago I sent him a poem." She paused. "It wasn't that complimentary. I fear he may not have forgotten."

Lady Huntingdon laughed heartily. "Yes, Mr. Occom told me about that. You have quite a penchant for sending your verses to strangers." She patted Phillis' hand. "I wouldn't fret about it. In spite of ruling a kingdom, their Majesties are quite human."

In preparation for the event, the Countess called in her

seamstress to design a gown for Phillis.

It was to be a white dress with yards and yards of skirt and a long train, fitted closely though the bodice, and trimmed with tiny pearls.

Phillis could hardly contain her excitement. Within days she was spending hours either at fittings or being instructed in royal protocol. Each night she practiced her curtsy and went over the rules she would follow in their Majesty's presence. Speak only when spoken to; do not ask any direct questions. She only hoped she could remember them.

"Don't worry about it," Lady Catherine said. " King George is a gentle man, and although the Queen has a vile temper, it is only when she is crossed. Just smile and be your charming self, and they'll love you as much as we do."

In the midst of all this excitement, there was something else. Nat was in love with Sally Thornton. Although he said nothing of any definite plans, Phillis knew the look. It was the same as Mary had worn when she met Reverend John. Just the mention of Sally's name put a light in Nat's eyes.

The book was published on schedule. Now, a week later, Phillis looked at it for perhaps the hundredth time. It was just as she had pictured it, slender and black, the title, *Poems on Various Subjects, Religious and Moral*, by Phillis Wheatley, lettered in gold. The preface read:

> The following poems were written originally for the amusement of the author, as they were the Products of her leisure moments, she had no intention ever to have published them, nor would they now have made their Appearance but at the importunity of many of her best and most generous friends; to whom she considers herself as under the greatest obligation.
>
> As her attempts in poetry are now sent into the world, it is hoped the Critics will not severely censure their defects; and we presume they have too much merit to be cast aside with contempt, as worthless and trifling Effusions. As to the Disadvantages she has laboured under, with regard to learning, nothing needs to be offered, as

her Master's letter will sufficiently show the Difficulties in that respect she had to encounter. With all their imperfections, the Poems are now humbly submitted to the Perusal of the public.

On the next page was a copy of a letter from Master John certifying as to her capabilities. Written as simply as he spoke, she had the feeling he was standing beside her as she read his words telling how her own curiosity had led to her writing; that the poems were entirely her own work.

A copy of the certification signed by the members of the Committee which had met to attest to her intellect brought back poignant memories. She saw again the wigged gentlemen sitting the length of the table. She had come a long way since then.

Lady Huntingdon appeared in the doorway. "Mrs. Baines is here for your final fitting." She smiled. "You look positively radiant today."

"I've never been happier," Phillis replied. "I don't deserve such blessings."

"Yes, you do. It is only right, for nobody has brought such joy into my life as you have since you've been here."

Phillis knew if she stayed much longer, she might never want to leave, for London was truly the closest thing to what she imagined Paradise must be. It was as though as long as she remained here, nothing unpleasant could touch her.

CHAPTER XXII

A WEEK LATER Phillis was in the garden when she heard Colette call.

"Madame was looking for you," she said when Phillis returned to the house. "Here is a letter for you."

Phillis was surprised at hearing from home so soon again. She opened it and began to read.

"Mademoiselle, you look so strange. Are you all right?"

Phillis clutched a nearby chair for support and reread Mary's words, as though they might change for the better.

Dearest Phillis:

It pains me to write such news, but both Father and Master John agree I must before it is too late. Mother was taken ill shortly after you left and has grown steadily worse. She can no longer rise out of bed, and I fear she may not live to see the baby. She is well taken care of, but pines endlessly for you. Each day she looks at your picture and murmurs, "My Phillis," and says to friends, "This is my youngest daughter, Phillis."

I know your health has improved there, but I cannot bear the thought of Mother never seeing you again. If you could find it in your heart to return home, we all agree it might give her the will to fight this illness.

I cannot tell you what to do. It will have to be your own decision. Please believe that both John and I pray it will be the right one for both you and Mother. God bless you.

Mary

The letter fluttered from her hand. Phillis heard Colette's frightened cries for help as the room whirled for an instant before she slumped to the floor.

She awoke to find the Countess leaning over her.

"Phillis, what is it?"

"The letter, Madame." Colette retrieved it and handed it to her employer.

"You poor child." Lady Huntingdon helped her into a chair. "Colette, fetch Mr. Wheatley at once."

Nat arrived moments later, his face white as he read the letter.

"If I'd only known..." his voice broke... "there wasn't a hint of this in her last letter, but that's so typical of Mother. The last thing she would ever want is to worry us on her account."

Phillis shuddered as she downed the spirits handed her. "Nat, I must go home." She paused. "But what if it's already too late?"

"Don't even think about that," said Lady Huntingdon. "We will put it into the hands of the Lord." She squeezed Phillis' hand. "I know she will be there to welcome you back. The knowledge you are coming will keep her alive."

Phillis wished she felt as confident. "What about you, Nat?" she asked.

"I wish I could go too, but with Thornton and Calif both at sea, I don't see any chance. They entrusted the business to me. There's just no one else."

Phillis turned to the Countess. "How soon can I leave?"

"I shall see to it Lord Dartmouth gets word immediately."

Lady Huntingdon patted Phillis' shoulder. "Now don't worry about a thing. After all, the Earl is close to the King, and if necessary I feel sure he can count on the Court's full support in securing prompt passage."

She bustled out, Colette following. Phillis buried her face in Nat's waistcoat, the buttons pressing sharply into her cheek as he held her close. "There, Phillis, cry it out. You'll feel better for it," he said. "What a rotten time for you to have to leave with the presentation next week . . ."

"Do you think any of that matters?" She dabbed at her eyes with the handkerchief he handed her. "Your mother is all I care about, and the sooner I'm back with her the better. I never should have left her." She struggled to control her emotions.

With Lord Dartmouth's help, she was ready to leave in a matter of days. She had said goodbye to Colette upstairs, and only the Countess, Nat, and the Dartmouths were with her as she waited for a carriage the morning of her departure.

The Countess kissed her. "I shall not say goodbye, dear, for I feel certain we are destined to meet again. In fact, I have discussed with Lord Dartmouth the possibility of a trip to Georgia to personally inspect the orphanage Mr. Whitefield bequeathed me."

"That would be wonderful," Phillis agreed. "Then you can visit us in Boston too." The thought made parting easier.

"Tell Mother I shall come as soon as I can," Nat said as he helped her into the carriage. She nodded, but she had the feeling she was seeing him for the last time. She felt tears on her cheeks as she waved one last time before they rounded the curve, then settled back against the cushions praying she would reach her mistress in time.

How different the return from her arrival. A thick fog had changed to a monotonous drizzle of rain, and she scarcely saw a thing as they careened over the cobbled streets and clattered over wooden bridges. The occasional clap of thunder and flash of lightning was appropriate to her desolate mood as the spires of London gave way to rain soaked country fields marked off by hedgerows like huge patchwork quilts.

Only on board ship, just before they lifted anchor, was she jerked out of her apathy enough to gaze at the green hills with genuine emotion, aware she was leaving a country she had grown to love.

She remembered little of the return voyage other than being thankful the winds were favorable so they made good time. She emerged from her lethargy only when they slipped past Lighthouse Island in the outer reaches of Boston Harbor. Her heart quickened at sight of the State House and familiar North Church steeple silhouetted against the scarlet and mauve shadows cast by the setting sun.

Mary and Reverend John were there to meet her. To her surprise, they told her Prince had asked for a release so he could marry a woman who belonged to another family. They had already moved to Maryland. And Dora, sent to help Miss Susannah's sister in New York, had liked it so well she had asked permission to stay permanently. Things were changing, Phillis thought. In answer to her anxious queries, they told her Susannah was holding her own, but nothing they said adequately prepared her for what she saw when she crossed the threshold of her mistress' bedroom.

The beloved face had a waxy texture, and there was a peculiar yellow cast to the whites of her eyes. Her white hair fell loose on the pillow, but the eyes sunk far back in her head shone with a jewel-like radiance as she reached her skeletal arms out to Phillis.

"My child, you've come home."

Phillis stifled a sob as she kissed the hot, dry face.

"I'm here now," Phillis soothed, "and you're going to get well." Taking only minutes to refresh herself, she sat by her mistress' side until she slept.

The family tacitly understood that Phillis had established dominance in the sickroom, and Susannah was soon responding. Although far from well, within a week she was eating better and able to sit in a chair for short periods.

The whole household was amazed at Phillis' newly acquired self confidence and her gentle but firm air of authority which caused Mrs. Birdwell to exclaim, "That ain't the same girl that went to England."

"Phillis, you've changed," Mary told her.

"Not really," she answered. "Except that I feel so much better."

"It's not just your health." Mary gave her an appraising glance as they went into the parlor. "You're so much more sure of yourself than you used to be."

"I'm not sure it's a good thing, Miss Mary." Phillis had been aware of it herself, realizing she now had a comparison to make between the life she had always known and what it could be if she were free. Each time she donned black dress, white apron, and cap, she was reminded that no matter how well the Wheatleys treated her, she was not a free woman.

Susannah continued to hold her own, and toward the end of the month, Phillis took advantage of a brief respite from her nursing duties to sit in the yard. She was about to go back into the house when a man she judged to be close to Nat's age walked jauntily up the street, paused at the gate, then pushed it aside and strode toward her.

Broad-shouldered and slim-hipped, wigged, and attired in the fashion of a prosperous businessman, his skin was a rich chocolate brown. Seeing her, he flashed a dazzling smile, lifted his hat, and bowed slightly.

"Miss Wheatley?"

She felt a sudden rush of shyness. "My mistress is indisposed," she said, thinking he had said Mrs. Wheatley.

"Miss *Phillis* Wheatley?"

"I am she,"

He brightened. "Miss Wheatley, I am John Peters. I have looked forward to making your acquaintance for some time." At her puzzled look he chuckled. "Surely you know, Miss Wheatley, that all Boston has heard of your trip to London and your reputation as a poet." He smiled. "I have placed an order for a copy of your book."

"Why, how kind of you." She was overwhelmed. She had been so busy since her return she had not even stopped to think about her fame spreading here at home.

"It is my pleasure to meet such a charming as well as talented young lady."

She felt the blood rush to her face.

Apparently sensing her embarrassment, he said, "Don't worry, Miss Wheatley. We have a mutual acquaintance. I'm recently from Newport, and Miss Obour Tanner asked me if I would be so kind as to deliver this to you." He handed her a letter.

She immediately felt more at ease.

"Thank you." It had been a long time since she had heard from Obour. At the end of the letter she found what she was subconsciously looking for.

> "...I am sending this letter by way of Mr. John Peters. He is opening a grocery store on Queen Street, and I feel sure you will find him a delightful person. I find him pleasant company and hope this will serve as an introduction. He reads and writes fluently and is much interested in your writing, so I feel certain you share a great deal in common."
>
> Your friend and sister
> Obour Tanner

"Thank you again, Mr. Peters." "My friend tells me you have opened a store?"

"Yes. I should be flattered if your mistress would consent to honor me with her business."

"I shall mention it to her."

"And I should be further honored if I might have the opportunity of seeing you from time to time. Perhaps you would read me some of your poetry?"

"I should like that." Sharing something with a man of her own race would be an entirely new experience for her.

"Until we meet again, then." He smiled at her, his teeth startlingly white against his dark skin. He was truly the handsomest man she had ever met.

CHAPTER XXIII

"Now THERE IS A BEAUTIFUL WOMAN, thought John Peters as he walked briskly toward Queen Street, and his mind shifted to the endless succession of women he had known ever since the age of thirteen, when he had lain with the first in the cotton field at the McLeish plantation in Carolina.

He hoped he had been right in coming to Boston. He was tired of running. So many years since he'd fled the McLeish place. He could still hear the shots ringing out, the hounds baying to the east, as he lay in the brush praying they wouldn't shoot him in the back like they had his Pa.

No matter that Pa had always yelled at him. Even that was better than the way it was afterward when nobody noticed him. He wished Ma would have yelled at him sometimes, but

he guessed she was just too tired between nursing and birth-
ing. Either one at the breast or inside her belly all the time.
He figured that was what finally killed her when he was
fifteen. After that, he'd lived only to make a run for it, the
festering hate inside him ready to burst every time he realized
she'd still be alive if it hadn't been for McLeish's greed for
more field hands.

There was one thing she had done for him. "Johnny-boy,"
she had said as she walked the floor cramped up with pains
just before she had the last one, the one that killed her in a
rush of blood. "Someday, somehow, get yourself free, go
north. Maybe there'll be a chance for you to do something
'sides work in the fields all your life."

He had thought he was free when he finally got clear of
the McLeish place. But he hadn't reckoned on what it was
like for a runaway slave to try and fill his belly. He had almost made it. He just hadn't seen the patrol in time.

They said he was in Virginia, almost to the Maryland line,
and that it was lucky for him Jonas Parson needed someone
to replace a slave he'd just buried. He'd gotten in touch with
McLeish and offered to buy Peters instead of sending him
back. McLeish was just as glad to get rid of a slave who
couldn't do anything right anyhow.

As far as owners went, Parsons wasn't bad. Never whipped
him except when he was drunk, which was about once or
twice a month at first. But John soon learned to welcome
those drunken sprees, for it was then Mistress Parsons would
come to his quarters, and they would spend the evening with
John first learning his letters, then reading books, and finally
putting his own words down on paper.

"John, if your skin was white and your hair gold, it could
be my George sitting there," she would say softly, and he
learned to praise the Lord their only son had been killed fighting Indians. For the emptiness compelled her to seek a sub-
stitute, and way off in the country like that there was only

John. It filled some of the void inside her while her husband drank himself to death; an emptiness John knew he could do something about if only he weren't black, but there was a line beyond which he could not cross. A pseudo-son she could accept, but he knew she would never sleep with a black man.

After three years Parsons died and she told him he was a free man, he was sure he would conquer the world out there, prove he was as good as any white man. He had learned well; he could read and write with a good hand.

But freedom was more symbolic than real, he soon realized. So long as your skin was black you were expected to sweep floors, unload docks, and be sent packing the minute a white came along even though he couldn't even write his name.

He did a little of everything. Barbering, but then he'd nicked a white man's ear, which ended that. He shined boots; worked in a livery stable. On to Pennsylvania, Maryland, and finally Newport.

That's where he'd met Obour. Funny about her. Right from the start she'd made it clear she didn't need a man the way most women do, but he'd hung around anyway. First woman he'd ever enjoyed talking to. She could read as well as he could and knew people like the black named Amos who'd helped burn the British ship Gaspee off Providence that summer.

"Where'd you learn to read?" he'd asked her soon after they met when she came to the grocery store where he worked.

"I was bought by someone who wanted me to read to his children. You think I read well. I have a friend in Boston who is a poet. Name's Phillis Wheatley. You ought to get acquainted if you ever go there."

John Peters liked Newport. He remained there although the jobs weren't much; more sweeping than clerking, but at least there was free time. Usually in the afternoons he could go off into the back room, and read. He'd gotten hold of books on law, others on medicine, and remembering Phillis Wheatley he had obtained a copy of her poems, a discourse on some paintings done by a slave named Scipio. She'd called it "To S.W., An African Painter."

But in the end he was forced to leave Newport too. He'd been reading the day a thief came in and made off with the cashbox. While the owners did not suspect him, they felt that he was totally unreliable.

Boston. That's where he'd go. Things were happening there. Boston may be exciting, he thought as he let himself into his small grocery store he'd recently rented. He was also thinking of the girl he had spoken with so briefly on King Street. She was the first real lady he'd ever met. Enough to make a man think of staying in one place.

CHAPTER XXIV

IN DECEMBER the three ships loaded with East India tea reached Boston. Citizens were advised that under no circumstances would any tea be permitted to land. A night watch was set up, the people were armed, and given instructions as to what to do should the bells sound. "Massachusetts must set the example for the rest of the colonies," called out the riders from the Committee of Correspondence as they rode through the countryside gathering support for their cause.

Freedom. Liberty. The words were being bandied about daily, mocking Phillis, for never had she felt herself so tightly bound. At night her tears were mostly for how little she could do to alleviate Miss Susannah's suffering, but she cried too for what she had given up when she left London.

From early morning until long past supper, she laid cold cloths on Miss Susannah's hot forehead, changed linens, read from the scriptures, and coaxed her to eat. A creamy custard, the choice white meat of a chicken, or still warm bread spread with fresh churned butter, but her efforts did little to slow the course of the illness which was relentlessly taking her mistress' life.

Only in the afternoons could she escape the musty sickroom, and that only because Mrs. Birdwell suffered from rheumatism, making it difficult for her to go out into the damp cold to buy groceries.

"You'll have to go, Phillis," she said, adding she had been going to that new little store on Queen Street. "That Mr. Peters is a real gentleman. Where he gets that fine produce, I've no idee, but Mr. Wheatley says it's as good as can be got and for me to give him our trade."

Would John Peters remember her, Phillis wondered, as she trudged down Queen. But just as she reached the store she tucked back a stray strand of hair and smoothed her skirt.

He was waiting on another customer when she opened the door. The smile he gave her was what any businessman might give a customer but the look in his eyes was for her alone.

She turned away abruptly to hide her confusion, feeling as awkward as a gawky child. At that moment she could not utter a word as she busied herself examining the day's catch of cod in the huge fish bin.

It proved the first of what went from thrice weekly to daily trips in an incredibly short time, the hour of the day she looked forward to from the moment she arose in the morning.

She marvelled at the way he had somehow managed to turn an ordinary, drab, 18 x 20 foot storeroom into an appealing small bazaar of foodstuffs.

Bottles of oil, barrels of ground flour, tubs of pickled hog's feet, tins of spices, things which anywhere else would be nothing out of the ordinary, yet, somehow here they became something more. A few bright feathers tucked among the displayed items, a silver bowl to hold sweetmeats, the tubs full of whatever was being harvested—squash and pumpkins one week, crimson-colored berries from the bogs the next, all arranged with an eye to color. And not all the spices were in the tins which filled the ceiling-high shelves. Peters had opened some of them, pouring a mixture into a kettle bubbling on the hearth in one corner so that the shop smelled like a bake-shop, enticing more than one customer out of the cold. Only intending to warm their hands over the glowing fire, Peters would soon engage them in conversation, and before they left they would invariably have bought something.

And there was Peters himself. Despite the heavy coverall apron he wore, the smudge of flour on the tip of one ear, he somehow managed to give the impression he had bathed that very morning. Whatever the reason, more and more Bostonians found their way to his emporium.

What pleased Phillis was that no matter how many customers were there when she arrived, Peters would greet her with a warm smile and make her feel she was somebody special. He never failed to inquire about her family, ask if she had written any poetry, even offering to lend her his copy of the latest *Atlantic* magazine if she had not yet read it. For those few moments each day she felt much as she had among her London friends; but each time she went to his store she found it harder to return to the dreariness of her mistress' bedchamber.

The month wore on. Offshore three ships sat at anchor,

sails profiled against the sombre gray sky. Onshore, nerves grew taut as the deadline neared. It was the thirteenth of December. In four more days the cargo could be seized for non-payment of duties.

Phillis found herself listening for gunfire as she tended Miss Susannah, who was in no condition to be moved should their worst fears materialize.

Surely the Governor would grant clearance in time. On Wednesday hopes surged, as a final appeal was sent to his home across the river, the same hopes dashed as his terse message, "Clearance Refused" was read in Boston.

People were stunned. "It's all a mistake," they told themselves.

All that night Boston listened for the bells to peal, the criers to call out the good news.

But, outside, there was only silence as the ships off Griffin's Wharf rolled with the tide. In desperation, a meeting was called for the next day at Faneuil Hall.

"God help us if it fails," said Master John.

CHAPTER XXV

THURSDAY MORNING'S RAIN failed to dampen the excitement that gripped Boston as people crowded into Faneuil Hall for the meeting.

John wondered what was going to happen as he closed up

for the day shortly before five o'clock. With Sam Adams at
the helm, there was no predicting which way things would go.

A blast of cold air hit him as he stepped onto Queen Street,
but at least the rain had stopped.

Several dockhands and apprentices greeted him as he
crossed Marlborough Street, where a crowd had gathered.
"C'mon, Peters. Whatever they've got planned in there, we
might as well be part of it."

A tumultous roar from inside the church drowned out his
reply as the crowd broke open the doors and burst forth,
knocking down several who had been standing on the porch.
"The harbor's gonna be a teapot tonight," they shouted as
they surged into the street.

"Told you was gonna be action," a burly man said as he
crossed to where John and the others stood. "Get you some
feathers and start yelling like Indians."

Indians? John wondered if he had heard right.

"Sure. We're gonna dump that tea right in the water. All
342 chests of it." His gold tooth gleamed as he grinned.
"Reckon we'll find out just how good tea and saltwater mix."

John felt his blood race as they crossed to a small blacksmith shop on Milk Street. Not since his slavery days had he
felt so full of fight.

The man applying burnt cork to another's face looked up
as John pushed into the shop. "Joining us? Good. We need
every hand we can get. Quicker we get the job done, less
chance of trouble." He handed John a blanket. "Here. Cover
yourself with this." He took a closer look, then grinned.
"Guess you don't need this," he said, indicating the burnt
cork, "but get yourself something to smash chests with over
there and whenever you meet another Indian say, "Me know
you. That's the password."

Back on the street Peters raced along Milk Street toward
Fort Hill. From there the mob headed to Griffin's Wharf in
a body.

At the rendezvous they were formed into three groups, one for each ship, and warned to be quiet. "Remember," said the "sachem" for their group, "our only job is to dump the tea, and we're going to do it orderly. No rough stuff. If anyone get's hurt, it better not be because of us. If we are quiet enough the Lobsters won't know what's happening until we're finished."

Luckily, there was only a slivered moon, not enough to cause problems. They formed in double lines and marched down Hutchinson Street brandishing their hatchets like tomahawks. Griffin's Wharf loomed up ahead of them as they turned into Flounder Lane.

The captains were not aboard. Peters couldn't hear what was said to the mates in charge. Whatever it was, they retired to their cabins with only feeble protests.

But looking down where there should have been water, John wondered why they were doing it at low tide. There was little beside mud to dump the tea into. "We should have waited for high tide," he said aloud.

"Can't," said their "chief," "The customs officials will be here at the stroke of midnight to seize the cargo. We've got to have the tea dumped and be out of here by then. Get aboard and start breaking those chests open, fast!"

Then there was only the clunk of axes, the ripping of the canvas as the "Indians" fell onto the chest, John hoped nobody missed their mark with an ax. At such close quarters he half expected to see blood at any minute.

Peters winced as he jumped into the icy water, shoveling the tea as fast as he could. It was like forking hay.

"Break those pieces up. There's probably still tea in there. Got to be sure there's nothing left to tax." The water was soon full of grotesquely shaped wooden fragments, the opalescent heaps of tea floating languidly, not out to sea, but toward shore.

It was eight o'clock when they broke the last chest and

threw it astern. "Now," someone called out, "everyone line up on the wharf single file."

John did not march back to Fort Hill with the others. He'd had his fun. He slipped through a small alley that took him to Milk Street and crossed over to Queen and home.

By the next day all Boston had taken up the chant.

> "Rally merchants, bring out your axes
> And tell King George we'll pay no more taxes
> No more taxes on his foreign tea."

John had never seen Phillis so excited as when she came into the store the next day. "Master John was beside himself," she told him as he weighed the items she had selected. "I've never seen him like that. He kept saying over and over, "No bloodshed, nothing lost but the tea." She looked thoughtful. "I wonder who the Indians were." She shrugged. They say even the ones who dumped it were so well disguised they would never even recognize each other." She paused. "I wonder if anyone I know was there."

"I wouldn't be surprised," John said, his tone non-committal.

Pride tempered by the chilling thought of reprisals, Boston waited.

CHAPTER XXVI

A SECOND WHEATLEY GRANDSON, William, was born Christmas Day. Reverend John strutted like any proud father with two sons to carry on the family name. Overjoyed, Susannah fretted about having to wait until the baby could be brought to her.

The winter passed in a monotonous succession of days and nights blending together with little to separate one from another. There was one bit of good news. Mess'rs. Cox and Berry, who operated the bookstore up the street, reported brisk sales of Phillis' book after an advertisement appeared in the *Boston Gazette Advertiser*.

And to Phillis' surprise it was also selling well in Newport, thanks to Obour. Phillis had never intended to ask her help, but she had finally written asking if some of her friends might be interested in buying it. They had indeed been interested, and as the money arrived with requests for more books, it occurred to Phillis that this might be the means by which she might buy her freedom someday.

Within weeks Susannah had grown so weak she could scarcely lift her head off the pillow. Each morning Phillis prayed for strength to enter the room. Nothing had prepared her for the torment of watching someone she loved die by inches.

Her book sat alongside the bible on Susannah's bedside table.

How glad Phillis was that the book had been published in time for Miss Susannah to see it. Each time she picked it up, she marveled at how long her mistress had worked to make it come about. Only since her return had she seen the letters dating back several years to Mr. Occom, the Countess, even to Captain Thornton, laying the groundwork for what was to come.

"Dear Phillis," Susannah said one day as Phillis finished reading. "I have asked the Lord so many times if I made a mistake in bringing you home with me that day."

"How can you say that?" Phillis cried. "You've given me so much to be thankful for. What would I have done without you?"

"I have wondered that more than you can ever know," Susannah replied. "But have I kept you too close to me? I can't help loving you as though you were my own, but was that selfishness on my part? Should I have left you free to be with your own people?" She shook her head. "I shall never know."

Soon Susannah was unaware of time. The family was not sure she recognized them as they held her hand, but they continued to recite the scripture verses she had never tired of hearing.

On that last day toward the end of March, the three who sat at her bedside scarcely saw the spring sunshine that lighted the room. They were oblivious to everything except Susannah's rasping breath, the death pallor over her pinched features. Towards evening, she roused momentarily and reached for Master John's hand. Tears coursed over his cheeks as he leaned down and murmured something that drew a wisp of a smile from her, and then she was gone.

For the next week, Phillis merely went through the motions of living, as though a part of her had gone to the grave with her mistress.

"Dear Obour," she wrote when she was finally able to take up a pen, scarcely able to see through her tears as she poured out her grief.

> "I have lately met with a great trial in the death of my mistress; let us imagine the loss of a parent, sister or brother, the tenderness of all these were united in her..."

Her only consolation was the knowledge her mistress was finally beyond suffering, but it did little to assuage the emptiness inside her. As she struggled to right her world she was thankful she had Master John to look after.

Now they all worried about Master John. He had always seemed so strong, but weeks after Susannah's death he still wandered aimlessly about the house, making no effort to return to his shop. Although Phillis tried to tempt his appetite, he merely picked at his food until his clothes hung loosely on his large frame.

Only when Mary brought the two boys over did he become more like himself. Both Reverend John and Mary begged him to close up his house and live with them.

"No, daughter, I must stay where I belong," was his unvarying answer.

If only Nat would come back; but before Mary's letter telling of Susannah's death could reach him, a letter arrived telling of his marriage to Sally Thornton. They were making their home in London.

As the weather grew warmer they were delighted to see Master John gradually begin to respond and finally, one May day, Master John returned to his business.

Phillis was grateful for the warm sunshine. The ordeal of the past months had taken its toll. The relentless coughing, the tightness in her chest were back. Now with Master John back to work, she could rest more. And there was a consignment of her books to be sent to Newport. Obour had written she had sold all she had. She would send them today. For the first time since her mistress' death she felt optimistic about the future.

As she emerged from her seclusion and began to mingle with people again, she found Boston a boiling cauldron of hatred ready to spill over at the slightest provocation. It had been five months since the tea dumping at Griffin's Wharf, months in which tensions had built up and smouldered, setting off one incident after another.

In the aftermath of the Hutchinson-Oliver letters scandal the once beloved Thomas Hutchinson was now hated by rich and poor alike.

Boston was like a small child waiting to be punished, wondering when it would come and how severe it would be. On May tenth, the answer arrived as the ship, Harmony, bringing the Boston Port Bill, dropped anchor at Long Wharf.

The Bill ordered the harbor be closed as of June first, blockaded by warships. This would mean the only way to bring in food or supplies would be from the inadequate road across the neck, the city's only link to land. The blockade would remain in effect until restitution was made to the East India Tea Company, and obedience sworn to the laws and authority of the sovereign state of Britain.

The inhabitants heard the news in stunned silence. Were those who predicted war right after all?

CHAPTER XXVII

1774

WITHIN WEEKS the sight of Boston harbor dying for lack of use brought tears to the eyes of anyone remembering the bustling seaport it had been. Ships sat idle the length of the waterfront, while offshore English warships lay like a ring of serpents ready to strike for the slightest infraction of the edict.

Dysentery struck down one family after another in the midsummer heat. Rich and poor alike fought the panic which came from not knowing how to obtain enough to feed their families as they trudged to market to buy what little was available, all haunted by the fear, of the neck road being closed off as well.

But the blockade proved merely the start. Beginning in June, Massachusetts was allowed no more elected representatives. No town meetings could be held without written consent from the Governor, and a decree was issued advising that all persons "disturbing the king's peace" were to be tried elsewhere, in England or any other place designated by His Majesty.

It was common knowledge that Governor Gage was just

waiting for a chance to arrest Sam Adams, his brother John, and John Hancock. Obviously, Boston was to be starved and humiliated into submission, the example by which Parliament meant to bring her entire colonial empire into line.

What gave her people the courage to stand fast was the response from other colonies. Within days of the port closing, carts and wagons bearing fish, oil, corn, and coinage poured in from neighboring towns. Pledges of support came from as far away as Virginia and South Carolina, and at the first Continental Congress meeting in Philadelphia, Patrick Henry thundered to the assembled delegates, "I am not a Virginian but an American," while George Washington from Virginia had been heard to say he would personally raise one thousand men and march north to save Boston if need be. Throughout the colonies church bells tolled, and people made time for prayer and fasting on behalf of their sister colony.

Susannah's old spinning wheel came out of retirement as Phillis and Master John went about the increasingly grim business of obtaining the necessities of life. Under Mary's tutelage Phillis learned to operate it, taking pride in the fact that each day her total of linen knots increased. Clumsy at first, she began to enjoy it as she and Mary carded, bleached, and spun the skeins with which to weave clothing and linens.

She was enjoying a new found closeness with Mary as each drew closer to the other to ease the emptiness left by Susannah's death. Even with Master John she felt more at ease. Before Susannah's death she had felt the servant-master barrier with all except her mistress, but now it was as though the struggle to survive the seige had, if not erased, at least minimized the barriers.

Master John had been on edge for weeks. She knew it was because of money. It had created a problem when she used money from the sale of her books to buy food, but there was nothing else they could do for the shelves of his shop were bare and no other work could be found.

Now more than ever, Phillis looked forward to her trips to Mr. Peters' store. She liked his sharp mind, the way he kept her informed. "Have you heard the talk going around?" he inquired one day. "They say a group of slaves have gotten together and offered their services to fight against the colonials if the Governor agrees to arm them and give them their freedom."

His tone was casual, but she could sense something behind that inscrutable expression. She had the feeling she should phrase her answer carefully without understanding why. "It's probably just a rumor," she said.

"You're probably right." he shrugged his broad shoulders. "I saved these for you." He reached under the counter and brought out three large red apples.

She smiled. "I didn't think there were any like these left in Boston."

"There aren't many, but what there was I commandeered for my favorite customer."

"Thank you." She handed him the items she had selected and carefully counted out the coins to pay for them. If only that last shipment of books could have arrived before the blockade. She was suddenly aware of Peters' almost animal-like magnetism as they stood separated only by a narrow counter. "It's late," she stammered. "I must be getting on. Thank you for the apples, Mr. Peters."

His eyes danced as though he knew exactly why she was flustered. "I'll look for you tomorrow. Your visits, Miss Wheatley, are the highlight of my day."

In December, Mary was delivered of a healthy baby girl, promptly named Jane, and shortly after the first of the year Master John received a letter from Nat. He and Sally were happy, he wrote, the only flaw being they had not yet been blessed with an heir.

Spring came early, the snow long gone, the grass already green by mid-April. Phillis was readying the garden for planting, when the Lathrop's hired girl pounded on the Wheatley door. "Mr. Wheatley, Phillis, come quick."

Phillis wiped her hands and started for the door. Master John stumbled downstairs as she opened it.

"Mr. John and Miss Mary sent me to tell you the British—they fired on the militia!" Nervous excitement made it impossible for the girl to stand still.

"Where?" asked Master John.

"Paul Revere and two others rode out last night to let them know the British were on their way to Concord." Her words tumbled out. "They hung lanterns in Christ Church—in the belfry tower."

"Where is the fighting now?" Master John asked.

"They're in Concord, and the British, they're coming this way. The militia's following them. One of them rode ahead to warn us."

"Dear Lord," Phillis breathed.

"My Ma says we got to git outta Boston," the girl said. "She says come over here and then straight home so we can git to Worcester 'fore there's fighting right here in the street. I got to go." She skittered off.

Phillis closed the door and leaned against it. "Will many people leave?" she asked.

Master John nodded. "Those who are fortunate enough to have relatives in outlying towns." He paused. "I wonder if it won't be safer here. I doubt there's any danger if we stay in our own homes. At any rate, it would be difficult for Mary to go anywhere with a small baby, and I won't leave her."

Phillis glanced out at the trees already swelled with buds, the first spring flowers already pushing up through the moist soil. War seemed incongruous.

CHAPTER XXVIII

WAR. The people of Massachusetts learned first hand what it was like as Tory and Patriot alike experienced one common emotion—fear. The kind that clutches at one's stomach and bowels, makes the mouth go dry, muscles tighten involuntarily at the slightest unfamiliar sound.

Within days after Lexington and Concord the road out of Boston was choked with refugees. Wagons, carts, and carriages blocked the roads for hours while men, women, and children huddled together, their meager possessions tied in bundles. As many headed in as out of the city; for Tories fled the wrath of mobs in the outlying towns seeking the protection of British troops in the city, while Patriots sought refuge with friends and relatives in the country.

Master John worried whether he should change his mind about remaining in Boston.

"I think you'd be better off staying here," Reverend John told him. "The Tories plunder any vacated homes. So far, as long as we mind our own business, they don't bother us."

"Some say it will be over so quickly it won't touch us," Master John said. "At any rate, whatever comes, I feel better facing it in my own home."

"Do you have enough food?" Reverend John asked.

"We'll manage. There's still enough in the garden to keep us from starving, and we have a little salted meat."

Meanwhile prices soared. A loaf of bread formerly selling for threepence a loaf was now a shilling. Cheese jumped from fifteen pence a pound to two shillings, and corn was up to one hundred shillings a bushel.

Only shad, once known as "poor man's food," remained inexpensive. Both Phillis and Master John detested it, but it was food; and they were grateful for anything edible. As she strived to make it more palatable, Phillis couldn't help recalling the sumptuous feasts she had enjoyed in London.

Remembering brought a sharp surge of loneliness. With all that had happened, she knew there was little chance of her ever seeing any of them again. A spark of hope had died some months before on receipt of a letter from the Countess telling her the Whitfield orphanage in Georgia had burned to the ground. With that gone, the Countess would probably never make the trip to America.

As if war and inflation were not enough, smallpox had broken out in Charlestown, quickly jumping the river to Boston. This was not the first epidemic Boston had lived through, but there was a difference. Always before the well-to-do had escaped it by fleeing to the country, but now with the road blocked by Rebel troops, flight was impossible. Rich and poor were equally vulnerable.

By the end of May, the bells tolled for the dead so often the Governor ordered them silenced, feeling that it demoralized the population; but he could do nothing to silence the death carts rattling their way to the cemeteries.

The British Generals, Burgoyne, Clinton, and Howe arrived the second week in June, their mission to quell the rebellion. Within days, all Boston read Burgoyne's proclamation ridiculing the militia and magnanimously offering pardon to anyone who had participated in the rebellion—with the exception of Samuel Adams and John Hancock.

If his intent was to placate the people, the effect was just the opposite. It infuriated them.

It was no secret the British intended to fortify Dorchester Heights and Bunker Hill, which controlled the only entrance to Charlestown and "the neck." Days passed without any activity.

The moment came the third Saturday in June. One minute Boston lay in the peaceful cloak of pre-dawn, the next it was rocked by the roar of gunfire. What only the night before had been bare hills was now an ugly network of fortifications as ships bombarded the hills, flashes of light interspersed with puffs of smoke.

"They're landing on Bunker Hill." Master John shook his head. "How those Rebels managed to fortify it in one night, I'll never know. I wonder what Burgoyne thinks of our militia now."

Phillis' insides shook as she drank a cup of tea and fought to steady her nerves.

"I'm going back upstairs so I can watch what's going on," Master John said a little later. "Boston's never seen anything like this and probably never will again."

He reminded Phillis of a small boy with no thought of danger, while she turned hot and cold with every cannon burst.

Toward noon news was that the militia, instead of fortifying Bunker Hill during the night, had somehow blundered onto Breed's Hill in error.

Master John's pride vanished as he realized what that meant. "There'll be no escape," he said. "All the British have to do is surround the hill and the whole militia'll be wiped out."

He went back upstairs to watch the spectacle. Phillis finally succumbed to curiosity and joined him in the upstairs hallway from which there was an excellent view of the harbor.

The rumble of cannon rolled through the streets, and the sound of fifes and drums penetrated the air as lines of red-coated soldiers mustered in front of their tents on the Commons.

They watched twenty eight barges, their flags flying high, set off for North Battery, oars glinting in the blazing sun.

Once across, the troops lost no time embarking, marching in precise lines, their muskets upright. Over on Breed's Hill the Rebels waited in silence as waves of British marched toward them.

"Good God! They're burning Charlestown."

Phillis looked across the river. Balls filled with pitch crashed into the town from the direction of Copps Hill. A church steeple crumpled, the whole building a pyramid of flames.

"The whole town's made of wood." Master John's voice was grim. "It'll be gone in no time."

Phillis wanted desperately to ignore the sight but was held by a hypnotic fascination as she watched the flames spread from one structure to the next. From the first tentative lick of flame to the destruction of an entire building was no more than minutes.

Many, fearing Boston would be burned, had sent their family silver, portraits and all their valuables to relatives in Charlestown for safe keeping, and now were watching their own fortunes being devoured.

By mid-afternoon the British were advancing up the front of Breed's Hill like a wave of red ants while barges brought still more redcoats, until the approach to the hill looked like a blanket of blood. The air was still and unbearably hot.

They watched the Rebels hold their fire until the British reached the top of the hill. A moment later, a solid sheet of flame spewed out at the advancing troops. To their horror, redcoats fell like rows of toy soldiers.

Phillis could watch no more. Her stomach heaved as she realized she was seeing men die.

CHAPTER XXIX

SELDOM HAS A RETREAT evoked so much pride as the Battle of Bunker Hill; for although the British took the hill, the Americans inflicted three to one losses, miraculously keeping the redcoats from outflanking them and preventing their escape.

Scattered showers the day after the battle made it virtually impossible to distinguish gunfire from thunder. Differences momentarily forgotten, Tory and Patriot alike donated water and clean linen for bandages as the dead and wounded poured into Boston. Every available man was pressed into service, and since Reverend John had studied medicine before taking up the ministry, he did double duty. He not only worked side by side with the other doctors mending the wounded, but comforted the dying with a much-needed prayer.

Sadly, Boston assessed the toll the fighting had taken with no regard to rank or station. Dr. Joseph Warrens of the Provincial Congress and Caesar Brown, freed slave, died side by side in the same cause. The others who fought were mostly farmers and businessmen from Roxbury, Concord, Cambridge, New Hampshire, and Connecticut, all united as

Americans. Like every Negro in Boston, Phillis felt enormous pride on learning the shot that felled Major Pitcairn, the British Commander, was fired by none other than Peter Salem, one of the sixteen black men who had cast their lots with the Patriots.

By midsummer, smallpox and dysentery were rampant. It was a rare household without at least one member ill, and as though this were not enough, the scarcity of fresh fruit and vegetables caused an upsurge of scurvy. While the disease might not kill, it made life miserable for its victims, who were easily recognizable with their spongy bleeding gums, eyes sunk back in their heads, and the peculiar gait caused by tortured aching muscles. The delivery of fresh produce was effectively and relentlessly shut off by the British soldiers guarding the gates to the city.

Fortunately, both Phillis and Master John managed to escape anything more serious than an occasional disorder as they put their energies into finding enough to eat and praying that the British would not burn Boston. Phillis was thankful for John Peters; for their ripening relationship was one of the few things she had to look forward to these days.

Each time they talked, Phillis became more impressed with him. She had had so little intellectual stimulation since Susannah's death. Lately he had formed the habit of coming by evenings, and they would read poetry together.

"You're so beautiful, Phillis," he said to her one evening.

She hoped she looked more poised than she felt. This was a new experience for her. It pleased and frightened her at the same time.

"I wonder," he said, "how you manage to write so knowingly about things like love and God, and death when you know so little about life yourself."

She bristled. "What do you mean by that?"

He took her hand in his and kissed it. "You are a child when it comes to living."

"What a thing to say. I've lived twenty one years."

"Have you?" he shot back. "Really lived, I mean?" He shook his head, his eyes amused. "Phillis, you are like a bud in the springtime. Someday you will reach full flower, but it will take time." He let go her hand and leaned back. "I wonder," he said softly, "have you ever suffered?"

"Of course I have. I lost my mistress."

"We've all lost someone we loved, but what is that compared to what the rest of us have gone through?" She tried to look away, but he would not allow it, his eyes demanding her full attention. "Didn't you once tell me you remember nothing of your capture?"

She nodded.

"Obour remembers, and I remember," he said quietly. "Oh, how I remember those slave markets. The weighing rooms. Do you know what they do there? They feel a man's muscles, because that's how they judge what he's worth. Not his head, just those goddamn muscles. And do you know how they judge the women? Their breasts. The bigger the better. And with children it's their teeth. Doesn't that give you a glorious feeling, Miss Wheatley, to know you were shipped over here because you had the right kind of teeth? You think you've suffered? Let me tell you about being chained to a wall, beaten until you can't stand up. What do you know about life, you with your little belly full, your warm bed, and that woman who bought not only your body but your soul as well?"

She gasped.

"Did you ever stop to think what it has done to you? You're not white, you're black but you're not one of us either."

It was as though Sukey had somehow emerged from the past and was sitting here beside her now. She again heard the words spoken so long ago, "Trouble is, you don't really fit nowhere."

She attempted a sharp retort, then realized his mood had changed in the fraction of a second. Where his eyes only moments before had burned, they were now dark and mysterious, shutting her out completely. "John?" she said tentatively.

"Forgive me, Phillis. I got lost in my own thoughts." Suddenly his face was as open as it had been inscrutable seconds before. It was almost as though she had imagined it. A warning stirred inside her; but moody or not, she liked him better each time she saw him. She felt the tears welling up.

"You're crying," he said reproachfully. "Did I upset you that much?" Gently, he wiped away the tears with his handkerchief.

"It's all right. It just made me think of something that happened years ago." Haltingly, she told him of her experience at the Fitch home so long ago. "You're right," she said slowly. "I never have fit anywhere."

With his arms around her, she felt much as she had when Sukey was alive, that someone stood between her and the world out there.

"He is a clever young man, complacent and agreeable, and above all he is a gentleman," she wrote to Obour a fortnight later.

But there were others who felt differently. Accounts of his erratic work patterns followed him to Boston. "He's lazy, arrogant, thinks he's too good to hold down a job," the gossips said. Phillis disregarded everything she heard about him, except when she heard he was reported to have studied doctoring.

"Have you studied medicine?" she asked one evening as the two of them sat in the Wheatley garden.

"No," He laughed when she told him that was the current rumor. "I suspect it's because I patched up more than one in my barbering days," he said. "I haven't studied to be a doctor." He paused. "But I have started to read the law."

"You have? That's marvellous. Do you intend to go on with it?"

"If I get a chance. Unfortunately, I can't find anyone who'll provide me with a living so I can go to Harvard, but I plan to study to be able to defend our own kind." His eyes began to glow with an intensity she had never seen before. "Yes, Maam, John Peters is going to practice law, and then do you know what is going to happen?"

She shook her head.

The perfume from the flower beds and a faint stirring inside her made the moment sensuous. She was acutely aware of his overpowering magnetism as he sat close to her.

"I'm going to fight for our people, Phillis." His eyes burned like hot coals. "I'll show the world they can't put us down, mistrust us like they do. When I walk into that courtroom everyone's going to know the black man's got someone who's not afraid to speak out for him, and let the world know we're human beings even if our skin isn't white."

But even as she thrilled to his words, his outburst stopped. "Sorry," he said, his voice once again gentle. "I didn't mean to get so serious. Come, read to me."

She trembled inside as she opened the book on her lap. John leaned back, his eyes closed, visibly content as she began to read. She was half way through a poem when his arm crept around her shoulders. He was silent for a moment when she finished, then slowly deliberately, he took the book from her and laid it on the grass, then gathered her in his arms. His lips brushed her throat then rose to meet her lips. Incredibly, she felt herself respond, reveling in the feel of his taut body against hers. Then, stunned, she broke away. "John Peters . . . what if my master sees us like this?"

"He'd probably think it was about time." He grinned. "I had a wager with myself you had never been kissed. Now I know. Admit it, you liked it, didn't you?"

Before she could answer, he gave her a quick prim peck on

her cheek and bounded off, leaving her with a heart pounding like it never had before.

By midsummer, the focus of criticism shifted from the Battle of Bunker Hill to General Washington, who had assumed command of the Continental Army in July.

"I heard," Phillis said to John Peters one day, "Reverend John say that there aren't many men who would take on a job like that, that the army was so disorganized it was a miracle there were any men left to command. He said if they hadn't appointed Washington when they did, the men would all have gone home to work their farms."

"Washington?" John sneered. "He's one of those slave owning bastards. Havn't you heard he won't allow any Negroes to serve in the Army? Claims we'll form conspiracies against him." He snorted. "We're good enough to pick crops in his fields under a hell hot sun but not good enough to fight with him. Anyway, if I fight for anyone's freedom it's damn well going to be my own." He paused. "Of course, we're not the only people he looks down on. I hear he thinks only men with the proper family background are fit to be officers. "Gentlemen of fortune and reputable families generally make the best officers," he quoted mincingly. "By God, for every fancy dressed officer on Bunker Hill there were a hundred farmers and storekeepers doing the dirty work."

Phillis wished she had never brought the subject up.

Toward the end of August, General Gage was recalled to England, reportedly because of Bunker Hill. While waiting for his successor, he clamped an iron fist on Boston. Firewood became as scarce as food, as troops chopped down fences, trees, anything that would burn. Even the pews in Old South Church were sacrificed, and to the town's horror, John Lathrop's church was torn down and burned for fuel.

The summer finally burned itself out as the days shortened, the maples turned scarlet, and the birches yellowed. Except for sporadic exchanges of gunfire, the war was at a standstill. The Continental Army sat in Cambridge while the British drilled on the Commons and commandeered all the food they could get their hands on, sharing it only with Loyalists. Both sides were running out of patience. The farmers had never dreamed they would be out of their fields this long, while the British had fully expected to be home months before.

General Gage sailed for England the tenth of October and was replaced by General Howe. The talk against Washington continued. Strange how she had come around so positively to the Patriot side. It was no sudden thing, rather a gradual change in her thinking. It had started in London, where she could see both sides, but it wasn't until after her return to Boston that the idea of freedom had grown to a flame inside her and the word liberty had taken on a dual meaning. Might her country's freedom coincide with her own?

Just today she had heard someone say, "Washington can't handle the Revolution. No Southerner can. Why didn't they put our Hancock in there? He'd never watch us suffer like this."

But Phillis remembered Mary saying long ago that Hancock was an arrogant pompous man, more interested in John Hancock than any cause. They were wrong about Washington. Anyone who studied history knew God had always sent someone at the moment he was needed. She was sure providence hadn't let them down this time. How all this criticism must hurt Washington. If only she could do something to show him how she felt.

There was something she could do. For the first time in many months she picked up a pen and began to write.

She wrote rapidly. Thoughts whirled through her head so fast she was afraid she might not be able to capture them all. She reviewed the positive things she had heard about Washington. The modest way he had accepted his command, the journey from Philadelphia over muddy roads. She must set them all down.

It had grown dark, and the first night stars were visible as
she wrote the last lines:

> To His Excellency General Washington
> Celestial choir! enthron'd in realms of light,
>   Columbia's scenes of glorious toils I write.
> While freedom's cause her anxious breast alarms,
> she flashes dreadful in refulgent arms.
> She mother earth her offspring's fate bemoan,
> And nations gaze at scenes before unknown!
> See the bright beams of heaven's revolving light
> Involved in sorrows and the veil of night!
>   The goddess comes, she moves divinely fair,
> Olive and laurel bind her golden hair:
> Wherever shines this native of the skies,
> Unnumber'd charms and recent graces rise.
>   Muse! bow propitious while my pen relates
> How pour her armies through a thousand gates,
> As when Eolus heaven's fair face deforms,
> Enwrapp'd in tempest and a night of storms;
> Astonish'd ocean feels the wild uproar,
> The refluent surges beat the sounding shore;
> Or thick as leaves in Autumn's golden reign,
> Such, and so many, moves the warrior's train.
> In bright array they seek the work of war,
> Where high unfurl'd the ensign waves in air.
> Shall I to Washington in praise recite?
> Enough thou know'st them in the fields of fight.
> Thee, first in place and honours,—we demand
> The grace and glory of thy martial band.
> Famed for thy valour, for thy virtues more.
> Hear every tongue thy guardian aid implore!
>   One century scarce perform'd its destined round,
> When Gallic powers Columbia's fury found;
> And so may you, whoever dares disgrace
> The land of freedom's heaven-defended race!
> Fix'd are the eyes of nations on the scales,
> For in their hopes Columbia's arm prevails
> Anon Britannia droops the pensive head,
> While round increase the rising hills of dead.

Ah! cruel blindness to Columbia's state!
Lament thy thirst of boundless powers too late.
    Proceed, great chief, with virtue on thy side,
That ev'ry action let the Goddess guide.
A crown, a mansion, and a throne that shine,
With gold unfading, WASHINGTON! be thine.

There. She read it over, satisfied it conveyed what she felt,
that he was commander by destiny, his power of the almighty, and their cause a just one.

The candle sputtered as she took a fresh sheet of paper and
wrote:

October 25, 1775

Sir.
    I have taken the freedom to address your Excellency in
the enclosed poem and entreat your acceptance, although
I am not insensible of its inaccuracies.
    Your being appointed by the Grand Continental Con-
gress to be Generalissimo of the Armies of North America
together with the fame of your virtues excites sensations
not easy to suppress. Your generosities, therefore, I pre-
sume will pardon the attempt. Wishing your Excellency
all possible success in the great cause you are so gener-
ously engaged in, I am
        Your Excellency's Most Obedient Humble Servant
                Phillis Wheatley

She folded the papers together, and sealed them. Tomorrow
she would try to find someone to take it across the river to
Cambridge.

CHAPTER XXX

THE WAR FLICKERED ON half-heartedly. General Washington responded to complaints of inaction by dispatching a force to Canada under the leadership of General Benedict Arnold. In November, patriots were jubilant on hearing he had joined forces with General Montgomery, who was in Montreal. Together, the two generals and their men were pushing on to Quebec.

Although many still hoped for reconciliation, those hopes were dashed with the news that the King had announced his intention to smash the rebellion by force, hinting that foreign powers were ready to assist England.

In January, the British still held Quebec, and in the battle to take it, Montgomery was killed and Arnold wounded. Reports trickled in that because the Americans had been forced to attack before they were ready, combined with bad weather and disease, it had cost them the campaign.

Boston was soon like a tomb of living dead. Both Phillis and Master John took to staying in bed until mid-morning, huddling under the quilts for warmth. In an effort to conserve precious firewood they closed off all but the kitchen and two bedrooms. They stuffed rags and newspapers around the windows in an effort to keep in as much heat as possible. Water left in pitchers overnight had to be thawed before it could be used.

It was late in February when Phillis heard a horse clatter up the street and stop in front of the house.

The boy on the doorstep was dressed in shabby homespun, his fair hair tied back in a queque. "Is this the home of Mr. John Wheatley, and does a Miss Phillis live here?" he asked.

She opened the door wider. "This is Mr. Wheatley's home, and I am she. What do you want?"

"I have a letter from Cambridge." He took it out of the pouch slung loosely over one shoulder, handed it to her, and was gone.

She was puzzled. She knew no one in Cambridge.

She unsealed it and began to read, then rushed to where Master John was warming his hands by the fire. "Here, read this. I can't believe it."

"Cambridge, February 28, 1776," he read aloud.

CAMBRIDGE, *Feb.* 28, 1776.

MISS PHILLIS—

Your favor of the 26th of October did not reach my hands till the middle of December. Time enough, you will say, to have given an answer ere this. Granted. But a variety of important occurrences, continually interposing to distract the mind and withdraw the attention, I hope will apologize for the delay, and plead my excuse for the seeming but not real neglect. I thank you most sincerely for your polite notice of me in the elegant lines you enclosed: and however undeserving I may be of such encomium and panegyric, the style and manner exhibit a striking proof of your poetical talents; in honor of which, and as a tribute justly due to you, I would have published the poem had I not been apprehensive that, while I only meant to give the world this new instance of your genius, I might have incurred the imputation of vanity. This, and nothing else, determined me not to give it place in the public prints.

If you should ever come to Cambridge, or near headquarters, I shall be happy to see a person so favored by
the Muses, and to whom nature has been so liberal and
beneficient in her dispensations. I am, with great respect,
your obedient, humble servant,

GEO. WASHINGTON.

She shook her head as though to clear it. "Master John,"
she said when she could speak, "I can't believe what I've just
read. Surely the Commander of the Continental Army would
not write someone like me much less invite a slave to visit. It
must be a prank."

"I would be inclined to agree save for the fact that you
have visited others as distinguished. The General must know
of your trip to London, your book." He paused. "We must
find a way for you to go to Cambridge."

She shook her head. "It's out of the question." She looked
at the signature again. "Much as I'd like to, I'm sure he is
too busy to spare the time. Just the letter is something I shall
always treasure." She paused. "I wonder what Mary and Reverend John will say when we tell them."

"We shall show it to them this afternoon. We must exercise
caution, though. It might not be wise to let many know of
this. The town is flooded with Tories, and I hate to think
you might come to harm over this." His usually bland eyes
flashed with anger. "Damn the conditions that have brought
us to this. If it means we can be free to think and say what
we believe, the price is worth it."

Phillis had never seen Mary so excited as when she read
the General's letter. Reverend John and the boys crowded
around to see it.

"Phillis, you must go," Mary exclaimed.

"I agree. We'll find a way." There was just the suggestion
of a smile on Reverend John's face. "The Lord will provide,"
he murmured mysteriously.

They were awakened by cannon fire that night, and for

three more as the British and American forces traded fire hour by hour. Phillis tossed and turned, her stomach turning over at each fulminating crash that told a shell had hit its mark.

On Tuesday morning she looked out to see Dorchester Heights fortified. So that was what Washington had been doing while the guns blazed away.

Reverend John shook his head. "I'm afraid our troops are in for a fight they're not ready for. No matter how well Washington has trained them, they're still raw recruits, nothing compared to the British. On top of that, the river's a mile wide where they'd have to cross. They'll be landing right in the face of Howe's cannon."

His eyes darkened. "I've seen enough of the victims they bring in to know what these men face when they go into battle. After a day of seeing them I wonder if there will be one whole man left in Massachusetts by the time it is over."

"Where is it you're off to this morning?" Master John asked.

"Cambridge. One of my parishioners is ill in Washington's camp, and they've sent for me." He started for the door. "While I'm there I'll work on getting you that visit, Phillis."

A storm blew itself out the next day, but the rough waters made maneuvering impossible. Three days later, Howe's men crossed back into Boston.

His order to evacuate took the town by surprise.

"No one knows what made him do it," said Master John, "but he's in a ticklish spot with those big guns aimed at him. On the other hand, he could burn the city if he wanted to. My guess is that it's a mutual agreement. Washington won't bombard the city if Howe'll agree to get out without destroying it." He paused. "And thank God for that."

It was an afternoon in March, four months before independence was declared that Mary knocked at the Wheatley door. "Phillis," she called, "I have news for you."

Mary was hatless, her hair flowed freely over her shoulders, and her thin cape was little protection against the stiff March breeze blowing in off the harbor.

"John returned from Cambridge yesterday." The words tumbled out so fast Phillis had to strain to catch them: "You're going day after tomorrow to see General Washington."

"I'm what?"

"To visit General Washington." Mary was patient, as though talking to a small child, for Phillis was speechless. "Well," Mary prodded. "What do you think? Isn't it exciting?"

"I'm worried about how I'm going to get there," Phillis said. "I hear coachmen are scarce. Mr. Peters tells me they've either fled to the country or joined up with the Army."

"I know, but my John's found one. He's been with a family in his parish for years, and he's agreed to take you. Come on, Phillis," she entreated, "let's go upstairs and find you something to wear."

CHAPTER XXXI

PHILLIS RESTED against the padded cushions of the coach and tried to collect her thoughts. She could scarcely believe she was actually on her way to Cambridge; but after a hectic morning during which she must have brushed her hair fifty times, she was in the Sutton carriage with their driver, Moses, perched up on the high front seat, guiding the dappled horses through the congested streets.

The three days since General Howe's order for troops and Loyalists to evacuate the waterfront could only be described as total confusion. From Long Wharf clear beyond Copps Hill, ships' masts formed weird abstract patterns against the cerulean sky. Guarded by warships that hovered like protective hens, there were big ships, small ones, anything that could be pressed into service—sloops, frigates, schooners, even landing barges.

The streets resembled a maze of anthills, everyone scurrying in different directions. Redcoats intermingled with civilians—men, women, old and young, children,—their possessions loaded into valises, carryalls, whatever would hold a few items. The fortunate few who had wheelbarrows or carts trundled them toward the docks. Up and down the wharves women sat atop bulky bundles, guarding them while their men went back for more. A child scampered by gripping a mangy looking cat. A woman minced behind her, a lamp clutched under one arm, a portrait under the other.

The tents were down on the Commons, although soldiers still milled around, and great piles of equipment had not yet been moved. Washington's guns stared down at them from Dorchester Heights, a sporadic burst of fire every so often serving to remind them who was in control of the city.

It became more pleasant riding through the undulant green hills as they moved outside the city. If it weren't for the harbor, one could almost forget a war was being fought, at least until they came abreast of the American camp just outside Cambridge. Here, in what were once spacious meadows, stood makeshift tents and shacks. No two looked alike. Some were made of sticks and stones, others dirty sailcloth, com-

binations of bricks and boards—anything which served the
purpose.

She stared curiously at the men, dirty and unshaven, dressed
more like hunters than soldiers. The stench was overwhelming.

She drew back as mud splattered on the window. They
careened across the wooden bridge which spanned the Charles
River and slowed as they entered the main part of town. She
was impressed with the lovely old homes set back amid towering trees. They gave an air of serenity to the wide spacious
streets, so unlike Boston's narrow winding ones.

General Washington's headquarters were in the Vassal
House, whose owners had fled months before. It was a large
cream colored construction set back amidst young elm trees,
dark shutters lined up like sentinels across the front. Phillis'
heart beat faster as she adjusted the puff of lace Mary had
sewn into the neckline of her dress.

Several soldiers stood clustered near the entrance. The
tallest spoke to Moses, then opened the carriage door, looked
in and spoke to Phillis. "The General is expecting you. Come
with me."

When they reached the entry hall, he said, "General Washington's man will be with you in a moment."

To her left she glimpsed a huge parlor, its windows overlooking the front lawn. To her right was a closed door.

"Miss Phillis?" The voice belonged to a round little mulatto
man, neatly dressed in a tailored black coat and buff breeches.
He wore a smooth wig with a tail in back tied with velvet
ribbon.

"I'm Billy Lee, Miss, General Washington's body servant."
His voice was a soft drawl.

He beckoned her to follow him. Just as he reached to open
the door she blurted out, "I'm scared."

He grinned. "No need. He's the nicest man ever lived."

General Washington was seated behind a massive mahogany desk, his wigged head bent over papers. It was such

a majestic setting she almost had the ridiculous urge to curtsy.

"Gen'l, Miss Phillis to see you."

Washington laid aside the documents. His coat was dark blue, bare of insignia with buff facings and glittering gilt buttons. Underneath he wore a gold waistcoat. His stock was white satin trimmed with lace, and he wore beige breeches. His smile was warm, lighting up the features which had seemed so impassive only moments before.

Why, he looks like Lord Dartmouth, she mused. It startled her to see how much the General resembled the man she had grown so fond of in London. The same long bony nose, wide-spaced eyes, full lips, and a chin that looked as though it was chiseled out of marble. A rare combination of dignified aristocracy and modesty which commanded instant respect. His eyes were kind as he said, "It is a rare privilege to meet one so talented and so kind to one of my years."

She bowed her head modestly. "The honor is mine, General." She glanced at him tentatively, then said on impulse. "I must say I find it much easier to write a poem to someone than speak to him in person, sir."

That seemed to amuse him. She felt herself relax as he bade her be seated. For fifteen minutes they chatted amiably about her work, her visit to England, and especially about Lord Dartmouth, then at a signal to Billy Lee he rose.

"Much as I regret it, I fear I must confer with my aide, General Knox." He sounded genuinely sorry.

She rose also, extended her hand, and said, "General, I want you to know that had I met you before writing the poem, I should have worded it the same."

"Thank you." He smiled, and for just a moment he looked more like a kindly grandfather than a General with the burdens of all the colonies resting on his shoulders. She left, reassured the cause of freedom was being headed by the right man.

Two days later, the mass exodus of soldiers and Tories

began. She could hear the fifes and drums as she walked to church. At the end of the street the last of the troops, filed aboard the large troop ships.

Behind them rushed the civilians onto the gangplanks, screaming and grunting, pushing and shoving each other.

By noontime, the docks were empty. Phillis watched as sails were hoisted. She gazed at the ships overflowing with people. She had worshipped beside so many of them, met them in the marketplace. The Fitches, the Sewells, the Brattles, Benjaman Faneuil, Quincys, Boylstons.

She turned back toward the house, stumbling over a coil of rope left on the walkway. She passed the Common, once more an open space, the grass trampled and virtually every tree gone.

It was actually ten days before Boston saw the last of the British, for they lingered off Nantasket Road just below Boston, giving rise to rumors that Howe might not be planning to leave the vicinity after all. But on the twenty-seventh, the strange armada sailed out to sea and headed north. Now Boston could turn its talents to repairing the damage wrought by the twenty-one month siege.

It was a gigantic job, for homes had been looted, furniture smashed, stores destroyed, windows shattered, and sometimes entire walls broken out for firewood. Families who had fled at the beginning of the blockade came back to assess the damage. A few were fortunate enough to be able to move right in; others had to find temporary quarters until damages could be repaired. But while it was hard work, it was done with the buoyancy that springs from hope, for at last ships could bring in what was needed.

"It's so wonderful to go to bed and know I'm not going to wake up to gunfire," Phillis said a week later as she and Master John lingered in the Lathrop parlor following Sunday dinner.

"Or something burning," Mary added.

"That it is," Reverend John agreed. "But we must remember this war is far from over. It has merely moved to a new locale. We must remember the people of New York in our prayers and never cease petitions for an end to this war."

It was well into July when rumors began circulating that the Continental Congress had issued a Declaration of Independence from England, making the colonies a free nation.

Independence. The word sounded strange. They had wanted freedom, but this was such a big step. It meant King George would no longer be their sovereign. It even meant Phillis' friends in England would no longer be countrymen. *It meant Nat as well.*

The rumor was true, but it was another five days before a public proclamation was made. Characteristically, Boston put its whole heart into making it a memorable event. On Thursday morning, the eighteenth of July, it looked as though everyone in Boston who was not bedridden poured into the square in front of the State House. What few soldiers Washington had left behind formed an honor guard. A complete antithesis of what Phillis had seen enroute to Cambridge. They were clean and well-dressed, their muskets gleaming in the sun. They stood proud and tall, a shining symbol of a new nation.

Phillis and John Peters were among those who listened to the Declaration.

> We hold these truths to be self evident, that all men are created equal, that they are endowed by their creator with certain inalienable rights, that among these are life, liberty, and the pursuit of happiness...

All men are created equal. Would there someday be a world where the color of one's skin made no difference? Phillis pondered this long and hard.

Pandemonium was the only word for the frenzy which

followed the declaration that "these United Colonies are and ought to be free and independent states . . ."

Bells rang, ships boomed salutes answered by a salvo from cannon high on the heights.

"Isn't this exciting? We're a free country," Phillis cried, looking at John Peters.

"I'll get excited when we're really a free *people*," he replied. "But you and I will never live to see it."

Why was he so cynical? Around them, total strangers embraced. He glanced at them, grinned, and his arms went around her as he lifted her up off the ground. He set her down gently, then his lips came down on hers with a kiss that lingered, giving her time to respond with an ardor she had never known she was capable of feeling.

"Phillis, I've never known anyone like you before," he said, obviously as shaken as she.

I love him. It was incredible, but suddenly, in the midst of the turmoil about them, she knew she wanted nothing more than to share her life with this man who challenged her whole way of thinking. How fitting that this new country should begin its existence on the same day she decided to embark on a commitment for the rest of her life.

CHAPTER XXXII

Boston was so caught up in the frenzy of painting and rebuilding that within months there was little to remind anyone of the devastation Howe left behind when he sailed for Halifax.

By September, the fighting was concentrated in New York, where Washington suffered two monumental defeats at the Battles of Brooklyn Heights and White Plains, sending the remaining Continental forces scurrying across the river to New Jersey. By the end of November, many prophecied that the American cause was lost. The British now controlled all of New Jersey, having driven Washington to the Pennsylvania side of the Delaware River near Trenton. The British were also within days of taking Newport, where they intended to spend the winter. Most believed the rebellion would be crushed by spring.

It was a grim December as they waited daily for the ominous news, fully expecting to hear Washington had capitulated. Although no one put it into words, everyone lived in fear that once again the King's vengeance would be directed against Boston.

But with the fighting so far south of them, there was less concern about the town being burned, and there was enough food. Smallpox had abated, and life on the whole was much improved. Phillis once again was worshipping at Old South Church.

A few days after Christmas, word was received of Washington's brilliant victory at Trenton, when he took advantage of the fact that the Hessians, the German professionals hired by the King to augment his forces who were great believers in celebrating Christmas boisterously, had consumed more than adequate portions of spirits. Taking advantage of their inebriation, Washington and his men crossed the Delaware during the night, and took them by surprise shortly after dawn, following it up by routing the British back to New York.

But by spring the picture had changed. Washington was beset by recruiting problems, the British received reinforcements with which to launch their march on Philadelphia, and the Continental Congress had fled to Baltimore. By October, with the Americans decisively defeated at Germantown and Brandywine, and the British occupying Philadelphia, there was talk of General Gates replacing Washington.

Although there was much she did not understand about the affairs of the new nation, Phillis liked having John discuss with her his future plans. She was proud of him. He had given up the grocery store and found a job clerking in the courts.

"I've had my bellyful of weighing out a bunch of this and a barrelful of that," he had said when he told her the news. There in the courtroom I can learn something every day."

During these past months, he had been accepted into the family circle by everyone with the exception of Reverend John. He said nothing, but his manner toward John Peters was cool, so subtle that only one knowing him well could sense it. It bothered Phillis.

Not so Mary. She openly approved of the romance.

"You are so right for each other," she told Phillis. "You've always needed someone with a mind that can match yours."

"Don't get any ideas about us," Phillis said. "I have my hands full looking after your father." She did not add what she was becoming increasingly aware of—that John was a free man, while she was still the property of Master John.

"Ask him for your freedom," John had said bluntly, but she didn't know how to go about it. After all, this was not the usual master-slave relationship by any means. And Master John would need time to decide whether to stay on alone or move in with Mary and Reverend John. Besides, Miss Susannah once said something about their having made arrangements for all the servants to be free once they were both gone. Phillis was sure of that.

She hummed as she dressed for church that third Sunday in March. John was going with her for the first time, and their appearance together would make official the fact they were "keeping company."

At sound of the door clapper, she took a last look in the mirror, biting her lips to make them redder, glad she had brushed her hair until it shone.

"You are truly the most beautiful lady in all of Massachusetts," John said when she greeted him at the door.

"And you, sir, are the handsomest man."

Her mood was buoyant as they strolled leisurely down the street.

"You look mighty happy," John commented as they turned the corner onto Cornhill.

"I am."

"Any special reason?"

She briefly considered telling him she felt that way whenever she was with him, but said instead, "I don't know. I guess it's just this beautiful spring weather and the war nearly over and all."

"What makes you think it's nearly over?" he asked. "And

even if it was, do you really think this neo-nation of ours is going to last much longer?"

"Why, John Peters, what a thing to say." They walked a few steps in silence. "You are a pessimist."

"Granted, but at least I'm realistic. I hate to disillusion one so naive, but do you realize we've set ourselves up as an independent nation when we have no government?"

"We have too got one. How about the Continental Congress?" She was distressed at the way the conversation was going, but she could see by the gleam in his eye as he warmed to the subject there was no stopping him until he had his say.

"The Congress is a little body of men who sit up there with absolutely no power to do anything." He half-smiled. "We're nothing but a bunch of colonies banded together because there happens to be a war. Once it's over, even if we should win, each colony will go its own separate way."

"I don't believe it."

He shrugged. "The fact is, every man in Congress is only concerned with his own special interest. Why, Phillis, it's less than two years since the Declaration, and already they've had one argument after another."

"There's General Washington. And men like John Adams and Thomas Jefferson."

"Yes, but Washington says he'll have nothing to do with the government once the war is over." He looked reflective. As quickly as he had launched into politics he relaxed and turned to her with a smile. "Enough of this talk when I'm with you." He reached for her hand.

She was glad he had decided to settle in Boston. Tomorrow she would ask Master John about her freedom.

Should she approach him before breakfast or after, she wondered as she put the porridge aside to cool the next morning, then glanced at the clock. He must be sleeping soundly. Ordinarily he was up and about before the fire had even taken hold.

Half an hour later she decided she had better see what was keeping him. Upstairs, she knocked at his door. "Master John?"

There was no answer.

She put her hand on the doorknob, then called again. A foreboding swept over her as she opened the door and went in.

He was still in bed, his eyes closed, and even from across the room she knew he was dead. How ironic that he had breathed his last just as she was getting ready to ask for her freedom. She felt a vast emptiness inside her as she realized she was without family; that this house where she had lived for seventeen years was no longer hers.

A few days after the funeral, she sat with the Lathrops in their parlor.

"What will I do, Miss Mary? I don't know whether your father freed me or not."

That was what must be determined right away, John Peters had told her on being informed of Master John's death. "I thought you were going to ask him."

"I was going to..." she had replied, feeling terribly inadequate.

"God Almighty, Phillis," he exploded. "Something as vital as your freedom, and you never got around to discussing it with him? Damn it, I wonder if you've got the wits to survive if you ever do get free."

"Miss Susannah said one time something about us being free after they were gone. I thought it was all taken care of."

"Thinking she has provided for you isn't enough." His tone was one of exasperation. "It has to be in writing. You don't belong to Mary now, you know. A husband owns whatever property his wife inherits. Legally you belong to Mr. Lathrop."

Phillis had tried to reassure herself that Reverend John was kind and gentle, and had always treated her like one of the family. She trembled now as they waited for Mr. Kentwater to bring the papers from the bank.

"Here he is now," Reverend John said. He admitted a wizened-looking gentleman in an elaborate wig and sombre black clothes.

"Good afternoon, Mistress Lathrop." He bowed slightly to Mary but merely looked at Phillis with curiosity, making no effort to speak to her. It made her realize that with Master John's death she was merely a slave; for her special status in the family had been in his and Susannah's hearts. She was not legally their daughter. Only Mary was considered a Wheatley now as they prepared to settle Master John's affairs.

Mr. Kentwater adjusted his spectacles and cleared his throat. "As you know, Mr. Wheatley was considered a man of considerable means. We all respected him, but unfortunately, since the war when he was forced to give up his business, he —like so many others—found it necessary to live on his reserves . . ."

"Come, get on with it." Phillis had never heard Reverend John's tone so sharp.

"The truth is, I am afraid your wife's father died in rather poor circumstances. I am not sure if he mentioned having obtained a loan against the house last year, for which the bank has not received one cent of payment." His mouth drooped at the corners. "I had warned him unless he could give them some money, they were considering taking appropriate action."

Mary's hand flew over her mouth. "Why didn't he tell us?"

Reverend John patted her hand. "Because he didn't want to worry us. It was typical of him."

Phillis listened to Kentwater disclose the amount of Master John's debts. She had known, of course, that the money was dwindling, but she had supposed there was still some in the bank.

"Then the only thing we can do is sell the house to pay his debts?" Reverend John asked.

"It is the only course I can see." Kentwater looked sympathetic.

"And the other matter I asked you to look into?" Reverend John said.

Kentwater shot a quick glance at Phillis. "I can find no reference to Phillis in any of Mr. Wheatley's papers. Legally, Mr. Lathrop, the girl now belongs to you." He stuffed his papers back into a pouch and rose. "I know you wish to spare Mrs. Lathrop the details of all this business. If you will come to my office tomorrow, Mr. Lathrop, I shall be glad to work out whatever arrangements we can come to regarding the sale of the property." He bowed to Mary and shook hands with Reverend John. "Good day, sir."

Mary covered Phillis' clammy hand with her own. "Dear Phillis," she murmured. "At least we have each other."

They installed Phillis in the children's room until another place could be made for her. She kept busy looking after the children, helping out wherever she could. It was a week later, as she returned from taking the boys for a walk, that Reverend John asked her to come to his study.

He seated himself at his desk. "Sit down, Phillis. There is something I must discuss with you."

"Yes, Reverend John? Something I can do for Miss Mary?"

"No, it isn't that. Actually you've been good for her. Just having you here has helped ease the sorrow of losing her father." He looked so distressed she resisted her impulse to reach out and comfort him. *Something was wrong.* She tensed as she waited for his next words.

"Phillis, you know how much we love you," he began. "We've talked and come to the painful decision we simply cannot keep you."

"I understand." She turned her head to hide the tears she felt coming.

"I'm not sure you do." Something in his tone made her look into his eyes. "You know how shocked we were to find Mr. ·Wheatley's assets gone? Unfortunately," he bit his lip, and she could see how painful this was for him, "that's exactly the position we find ourselves in." He shrugged. "It's something we prefer not to talk about. Nobody wants word getting out that he's poor, but the fact is, the church has been unable to pay me anything for some time now. We just cannot afford to add another person to our household." He sighed. "Besides, I can't help but feel that with your talents you will do better for yourself if you are free."

She tried to quell her panic. Freedom? She had wanted it, of course. Then why was she so frightened? Because, she told herself, you're your own responsibility. Nobody is going to see you are fed and clothed. And how would she earn money? He spoke so confidently of her talents. With the war going on, there were few people to buy books let alone anyone to publish them. Most of the printers and the booksellers had gone off to war like everyone else.

"Naturally, I am prepared to see that you have enough money to get settled," Reverend John said. "We thought perhaps you might be able to secure employment as a governess. I shall inquire among members of my church. Surely someone . . ."

She brightened at that, even though her practical side realized many people who would have hired governesses a few years ago no longer had money with which to pay one. Still, if she could hire out for merely room and board, it would solve her most immediate problem. And she still had a few more books left. Maybe she could sell them.

Reverend John smiled. "I hope you understand, Phillis, that we still consider you part of the family."

She nodded, forcing herself to smile. "I understand."

CHAPTER XXXIII

PHILLIS arranged cat-tails in a bowl and set them on the table. She had tried so hard to make the drab two-room apartment look more like a home; even with bright new curtains, it was far from what she was used to. But then, she was fortunate to have found anything she could afford. It was pure luck that this old commercial building, recently broken up into apartments, was owned by a member of Reverend John's church. Mrs. Lanahan had been skeptical of a woman tenant; but the fact that Phillis had belonged to the Lathrop family had made her reconsider.

Phillis sighed. A week since she had moved in, and she was still nowhere settled. The only corner that looked right was where she had put Miss Susannah's old winged chair, one of the few items not sold with the house, and arranged her books on the table beside it. Here, each evening, she would curl up and renew acquaintance with her favorite authors, always ending with scriptures from the Wheatley family bible which Mary had insisted she have. The books gave her a sense of security, as though she were still safe within the walls of the Wheatley library, untouched by the outside world.

She was glad John Peters had taken to dropping by nearly every evening. This evening he grinned as he stepped inside. "Look out there, Phillis. Is this a night to spend alone? Let's go for a walk."

They strolled leisurely through the warm twilight.

They talked of pleasantries as they passed the Hancock mansion and turned onto Joy Street. There was something about the way he was looking at her, the tone of his voice.

"Phillis, I don't like the idea of your living alone," he said abruptly.

"I don't mind. Anyway, if a governess job materializes, I won't be alone long. Reverend John thinks he may have one for me."

He reached for her hand. "Phillis, I want you to marry me." Before she could answer, he added, "Surely you must know how I feel about you."

"I—I don't know what to say."

"The important thing is, do you want to?"

"You know I do."

"Then it's settled. Phillis, I've wanted you ever since that day I first saw you in the garden."

They resumed walking hand in hand. She was so happy she wanted to stop the first passerby they met and say, "See? This is the man I'm going to marry."

"When do you think we should get married?" she asked excitedly as they turned the corner from Brattle Street.

"The sooner the better. How about next Wednesday. That gives you four days to get ready."

She burst out laughing. "But it's so soon," she protested.

"It's practical, isn't it? You have no family, and I see no sense in making a big fuss. I suppose you'll want Mr. Lathrop to marry us?"

"Of course. I must tell Miss Mary first thing in the morning." She stopped in the middle of the sidewalk. "What must be done before the wedding?"

"We go before the registry and get a license, that's all. We'll do it first thing Monday morning."

His long, lingering goodnight kiss made her feel protected and cherished as she never had before. She clung to him, reveling in knowing what it was to love and be loved. "I love you, Phillis," he said, his voice husky.

"I love you, John," she whispered, knowing one more kiss like that and she might be unable to deny him her bed even before the wedding.

"Phillis, whatever happens we'll have each other, and that's what's important."

She was still shaking for several minutes after he left. She watched until he was out of sight, then whirled around the room and blew a kiss out the window.

"I'm so glad for you, Phillis," Mary cried the next morning.

"Then you approve?"

"Of course I do. I want you to be happy, and I can see that you are." She smiled. "I've known all along this is the way it would work out. It's just that it is a bit sudden."

"Your father's death rushed things along," Phillis admitted. "I've loved John a long time, but I didn't know how he felt about me. It's strange, Mary, but I never can be sure I know what he's thinking."

"Do we ever really know what's inside another person's mind?" Mary asked gently. She jumped up, her face flushed with excitement. "My goodness, if we've only three days we must get things ready. You'll be married here, of course."

Reverend John was less than enthusiastic when Phillis revealed their plans and asked him to perform the ceremony.

"I take it you have given sufficient consideration to these plans, Phillis?" he said slowly, hands clasped together so tightly the knuckles whitened. "I don't like to pry, but since you have no family of your own, I do feel some responsibility for you."

"Thank you."

"I take it Mr. Peters has sufficient funds to support a wife? Have you discussed where you will live?"

"He is adequately paid for his job in the courts. He plans to move in with me as soon as we're married. There is plenty of room for both of us."

She had the feeling she must clarify whatever it was that had caused this wall between them. "Reverend John," she said, her voice hesitant. "I feel you disapprove of my choice."

"As a clergymen who has counseled for many years, I think I can sense your feelings for him are sincere, but I wonder about his ability to give you the happiness you deserve."

Resentment darted through her. What right had he to judge the man she loved?

He held up his hand. "In many ways Mr. Peters is a fine man. Certainly he has a good mind; but Phillis, I would be remiss if I did not point out to you that he seems to lack stamility; and that is the foundation on which marriage should be based. Love is important, certainly, but it does not pay a man's debts."

She had no answer for that.

"However, I may be wrong. I sincerely hope so." He smiled. "I can only pray your marriage will be a fruitful and happy one."

"Thank you. Then you will perform the ceremony?"

"Of course. I shall be happy to." He rose, indicating their talk was concluded.

He's wrong about John, She thought. *Someday he'll take those words back. He's just like most people. He only sees what is on the surface. He doesn't really know him.* But a small voice echoed inside her. *Do you?*

A few days later they stood before Reverend John in the Lathrop parlor. Phillis wore Mary's white satin wedding gown. Beside her John stood proud and tall, his new wig handsomely curled, his embroidered waistcoat catching the light so that it looked like jewels had been sewn into it.

Phillis glanced at Mary and the three children. The boys looked as though they were about to choke in their stiff collars, Janey adorable in ruffles and ribbons.

"Phillis, wilt thou have John to be your lawful wedded husband, to love, honor, and obey, and forsaking all others, keep ye only unto him so long as ye both shall live?"

"I will."

Later, in the apartment, John swept her into his arms. "At last, you're all mine," he murmured, nuzzling her neck. Gently he began to undress her. Her shyness turned to wonder and delight as her long suppressed passion rose to meet his, and the two became one.

CHAPTER XXXIV

NOTHING HAD PREPARED Phillis for the delight she found in being John's wife. The nights were pure bliss, each day one to be treasured as she threw herself wholeheartedly into making their rooms a real home. She was surprised at the pleasure she took in such simple tasks as planning meals and even stitching a sampler for the wall.

"You amaze me, Mrs. Peters. You have so many talents I never suspected," John would say on coming home and finding a new decorative touch. "But don't neglect your writing. That should be your primary concern."

And hopefully one which will bring in money, she thought, for prices were soaring higher than ever. John's pay did little more than take care of their most basic needs. If prices went up much more, they would be in real trouble. She had managed to put a few coins in the sugarbowl on the top shelf of the cupboard, but just last week John had demanded them to pay off a debt. She had watched him count them out until there were only two left.

She had reason to be concerned about the future. Just this past week, suspicion had become a certainty. There would soon be a baby. Late January or early February, she had calculated, and this was already August. She was thrilled. She could think of nothing in life more precious than a baby to hold and love. She looked down at her bosom, conscious that her breasts were larger than they had ever been.

"It becomes you," John had said emphatically the night before, when she bewailed the fact her dresses were tight across the bodice. "I like you that way. It makes you a real woman." He smiled. "You should've seen my mama. Hers were like watermelons. She was always wet nurse for some scrawny woman without enough milk."

She had blushed. Several months of marriage had not yet eliminated her embarrassment at his frankness.

As for the war, after three years of only occasional victories and several devastating defeats, Washington's army had emerged from winter quarters at Valley Forge to drive the British out of Philadelphia and back to New York, following it up with a brilliant victory at Monmouth, New Jersey, two days later. Even more heartening was the news that France had declared war against England and the French fleet would soon be bringing badly needed reinforcements.

"You're really happy, aren't you Phillis," Mary said one day in mid-September, as they sat in the Peters' sitting room sewing layette items.

"I'm so happy it sometimes worries me."

"Now that's an odd thing to say." Mary reached for another skein of thread.

"I know, but I remember how I felt in London." She paused. "I felt as though I was the happiest person on earth, and then suddenly it was gone—just like that."

"Nonsense. Nothing can go wrong now. You have John, and there's a baby coming. The war is nearly over. You're worrying needlessly." Mary smiled. "John and I were just saying last night you've had more than your share of sorrow, and we think God is ready to shower you with happiness from now on."

They both laughed. Phillis basked in the moment of close fellowship. Since Master John's death, she and Mary had grown closer, especially now that they shared the common bond of caring for a home and family. Mary was a combination sister, mother, friend, someone Phillis could turn to for any need John could not meet. But even after all this time, it was hard to disassociate Mary completely from her twin.

"Did you ever hear from Nat after you sent word of your father?" she asked abruptly.

Mary's eyes clouded. "No." Then she brightened. "Of course, it takes so long for mail to get to England. It's probably still on the way. I'll write again if we don't hear from him soon."

Phillis was about to comment when she felt a flutter low in her abdomen, then, as she was still wondering what it was, another. She was instantly aware of the child growing inside her. I, too, grew inside the body of my mother like this, she thought.

A week later Mary took to her bed with a severe cold. "It's

really nothing," she said when Phillis stopped by the following day. "All I need is rest. I'll be up and around in a day or two."

It was nearly dawn the next day when the Peters awakened to frantic pounding at the door. Phillis flew out of bed and groped for her banyan as John lit a candle.

"We're coming," he shouted. Phillis was right behind him as he flung open the door. Her heart pounded as she recognized the Lathrop's neighbor, Abner Smith, his clothes buttoned crooked, cloak flung loosely over one shoulder, and no hat. She caught her breath as she saw his usually florid face was drawn, his beady eyes bleak in the light of the candle.

"It's Mrs. Lathrop. Mr. Lathrop says come quick."

"At this hour?" John cried.

But Phillis was already gathering up her clothing. "Find out what's happened," she instructed John as she fled to the other room to dress.

She knew it must be a matter of life or death when she heard Smith say, "She's pretty bad. They've sent for Doctor Harris."

The Lathrop door was opened by Abner's wife. Wordlessly, she took them to the study, where Reverend John sat at his desk, head cradled in his arms. No words were necessary. They were too late.

"What happened?" she asked Reverend John gently. "She seemed a little better yesterday."

"She was..." his voice broke... "but then she woke up during the night...burning up with fever...I tried to bring it down...thought she was going to make it, but then she ..." he struggled to get hold of himself... "she just coughed up all this blood... then she was gone."

"The doctor never got here?"

He shook his head. "He sent word he was with Josiah Nelson's wife. Couldn't leave her."

Phillis knew his agony was a private thing, and nothing she could say would help at this point. "Do the children know yet?" she asked, her lips trembling.

He shook his head. "They're still asleep." A convulsive shudder seemed to age him ten years before their eyes.

"Would you like me to be with them when they wake up?" she asked.

He nodded, gratitude in his dulled eyes. "They're so fond of you, Phillis. Perhaps after I've had a word with the Lord I'll have the strength to talk to them about it. But what do you say to children when they've lost their mother overnight?" He looked at her, his eyes haunted.

She had never felt so inadequate.

"Here I am a minister who's been telling people for years what to say in this kind of situation, and now . . ." his voice broke again . . . "I find I'm totally incapable of facing my own children."

"You'll be fine once you've had a chance to compose yourself," Phillis soothed. It was strange having Reverend John, who had been the strength of the family for so long, the one they had turned to for counsel, like a small boy looking to her for guidance.

She left him and went to the nursery, where the three youngsters slept. Looking at them she felt a moment of sheer panic. Impulsively, she knelt and prayed for the strength she knew she would need in the days ahead.

She moved through those days in a veil of numbness, trying to take comfort in the evidence of how much Mary had been loved, as people poured into the parlor to pay their last respects. At Reverend John's request, she remained in the house when John assured her he would look after things at home. She spent most of the time keeping the children out from underfoot, telling them stories and playing games with them to keep their minds off the black clad mourners streaming in and out the front door.

Her worst moment had come the first morning, when Billy raised his freckled face and said in a hushed voice, "You mean she's like Grandma and Grandpa? She's living where we don't get to see her anymore?"

"Yes, but you must remember she's very happy there," Phillis answered.

"And she won't cough anymore or have to sit down in the middle of the floor 'cause she's tired?" Janey's blue eyes searched Phillis' face.

"That's right." Phillis was thankful for the faith which enabled a small child to accept simple explanations.

Their immediate curiosity satisfied, they seemed able to accept her going. I wish it could be that easy for me, Phillis thought more than once, for over and over, like a hammer beating at her mind, came the eternal question, *why, God, why?* Surely, if anyone was needed, it was Mary, upon whom four people depended. She was always so vibrant. It had been different with Miss Susannah and Master John. They had lived full lives, but she could not accept Mary's untimely demise.

She worried about the children, relieved to learn Reverend John's aunt Matilda was coming from Connecticut to help out. She remembered meeting her at the wedding, and had no doubt the elderly spinster would be competent.

"You will come visit often, I hope," Reverend John said. "You've been so much a part of the children's lives, it is important they stay close to you."

"Of course I will," she answered, but she knew even as she said it, things would never be the same again. Although Matilda Lathrop had been polite when they had met, there was a wall between them she knew instinctively would never be struck down; and was keenly aware that without Mary her life would begin to disassociate itself from the Lathrops. She would never be considered family again.

CHAPTER XXXV

IT WAS STILL DARK, but already Phillis could hear the restless squirming, the faint, pig-like grunts coming from the cradle. Much as she wanted to turn over and go back to sleep, Phillis knew she had better get up before Mary began to cry. John had been irritable enough lately without her taking a chance on his being awakened this early.

She picked the baby up, then, cuddling her in the crook of one arm, she seated herself in the old pine rocker and bared her breast. How she loved these quiet moments before the day began, when she could revel in being the mother of such a beautiful child. She was a few days past three months now and looked exactly like John.

She rocked back and forth gently as Mary nursed. She felt sorry for fathers. They were so far outside the special sphere she had cherished from the first day of conception. At birth Mary had been a stranger to John, but Phillis already knew her intimately, having shared every bite of food, every breath with her through those prenatal months.

As Mary sucked, Phillis let her mind slide back over the past few weeks, something she had avoided doing until now.

John had not been himself lately, and her attempts to draw him out had proved futile. They snapped at each other most of the time, and he was away from home more and more.

"It's normal with the first baby, dear," her friend Lydia Price had said last week as they walked home from church. "He's not used to the baby taking up your time. He'll get over it. Land sakes, you should have seen my Ezra when our first was born, but he was soon the proudest Daddy ever lived. John will be too. Give him time."

If only she weren't so tired. Bless Mrs. Lanahan. She couldn't have managed without her help those first few weeks after she delivered.

"You poor child," the landlady had said the morning she found Phillis in tears, Mary crying lustily, and the house in wild disorder. "Most women have family at a time like this. Good thing I'm close by."

"John helps as much as he can."

"Husbands are more hindrance than help at a time like this," Mrs. Lanahan had replied as she tackled the dirty pots crusted over with cold food. "What a new mother needs is another woman who understands."

Phillis had been sure things would improve once her strength returned, but three months later it was worse

"We never talk anymore," John had complained last night. "Either you're nursing the baby or getting ready to. Does she eat *all* the time?"

"I can't help it. Small babies eat oftener than husky ones."

"Go ahead and feed her. I'm going where I don't have to listen to a kid squall." He had jammed on his hat and slammed out the door. She had been too weary to care.

There must be more to life than this, she thought more than once during the next few weeks, for despite her efforts to quiet the baby and make things pleasant for John, he grew surlier than ever, his moods as capricious as an April sky. At least he came home every night.

The night he did not, she assumed he had been detained at the courthouse. At eight o'clock, she put Mary down and got out the china the Lathrops had given them for a wedding present. She added a vase of flowers in the center of the small table, then took a volume of poetry from the bookcase. They would read together after dinner the way they used to.

At nine o'clock, she set the stew on the back of the stove and went back to her needlework, acutely conscious of the slightest sound as she listened for his light step, the peculiar whistle that always signaled his arrival.

By ten o'clock, she feared something had happened to John.

John Peters kept his head down, trying desperately to quell the panic welling up inside him as he made his way along State Street. Not that he hadn't lost jobs before, but there hadn't been a family to support then. How was he going to tell Phillis?

Even though they'd been married more than a year, he still couldn't touch her without experiencing an overwhelming sense of awe. To think a real lady had married him. And to think he had once believed ladies were cold as marble. He smiled. She was no marble statue. At least until Mary came along. Not that he didn't love the kid, but she certainly complicated things. Even when she was sound asleep, Phillis was always the mother, listening, out of bed at the slightest whimper. How he wished it could be like it had been before, just the two of them.

But the baby could not be wished away. Anymore than he could undo what had happened this afternoon. *Damn.* This morning had started out like any other. And it might have stayed that way if he'd had the sense to keep his mouth shut.

He could only hope Judge Hayden would reconsider. The whole thing galled him. What had something that happened a month ago over in Brookline to do with his job here anyhow? They couldn't fire him for what he did on his own time, could they? But in his heart he knew they could.

But damn it, he'd read enough law to know injustice when he saw it. He couldn't stand by and see his old friend, Hotchkiss, railroaded like they were trying to do.

"He could have defended himself," the judge in Brookline had said, but any fool could see someone who stuttered that badly wasn't going to be able to say anything a judge would listen to. And John believed his story. If Hotchkiss said he didn't steal those chickens, he didn't.

John shook his head. It must have been fate that had sent him into that courtroom after he'd gone up to look at law books he'd heard were for sale.

All he'd done was stand up and say he was defending Hotchkiss. That damn fool judge didn't find out for a full two hours it was John Peters, law clerk, not John Peters, lawyer, standing there. He smiled. He'd done a good job. He'd convinced the court they didn't have enough evidence, and Hotchkiss was acquitted.

When you came right down to it, he had not broken any law. It was Hotchkiss who was under oath, not he; and when the judge asked who was defending, he'd merely said, " I am." He hadn't claimed to be a lawyer. It was only assumed.

What he hadn't counted on was word of the case getting back to Boston, or if it had, his getting any more than an admonishment.

"Sorry, Peters," Judge Hayden had said just an hour ago. "The court can only employ men of the highest integrity, and what you did in Brookline cannot be passed over lightly. I am afraid that, exposed to the courtroom the way you are in this job, the urge might manifest itself another time. Law is a profession, and nobody can just walk into a courtroom and pretend to be a lawyer."

Someday, John vowed as he took his severance pay and walked out, he'd show them he was as good a lawyer as any white lawyer.

But someday was not now. Hardly able to contain his rage, what he really wanted to do was cry. Instead he turned onto Fleet Street. King's Head Tavern was just ahead. He needed to fortify himself before facing Phillis.

It was nearly daylight when Phillis finally heard him. One look and she knew he'd been drinking, for his clothes were rumpled, his gait unsteady. But her anger subsided as quickly as it had come. He was safe. That was what really mattered.

"I didn't mean to stay so late," he muttered.

"Get those dirty clothes off and get some sleep," she said. "We can talk later."

How have I failed him, she asked herself as she picked his things up off the floor, hoping his snoring wouldn't wake Mary. Why couldn't he have come home instead of spending the night in a tavern? Why can't we talk to each other anymore? She made no attempt to go to bed but sat in the rocker until her full breasts told her it was time to feed Mary.

It was late the next afternoon before John stirred. Phillis' back was to him as he sat down at the kitchen table. He looks rested, she thought, as she turned to him. Better than that, she sensed he was ready to talk.

"I'm sorry about last night." His eyes begged for understanding.

"There must have been a reason."

He toyed with a spoon, obviously searching for words. "It's that damned Judge Hayden. He's been after me since the day I started." His eyes flashed. "If it wasn't for him I'd still have my job."

"What happened?" She set a bowl of applesauce and three corn muffins in front of him, struggling not to let her shock show.

"He banished me from the courtroom because he heard I misrepresented myself up in Brookline last month."

"Why would he say a thing like that? He must have you

mixed up with someone else."

"I wish that were the case," he said slowly. Her eyes widened as he told her of the trip to Brookline, about Hotchkiss.
"But that was no reason to discharge me. I did what I thought
was right defending one of our people who was receiving no
justice at all."

"It's all right. I understand," she murmured, "I'm proud
of you for helping your friend."

It was a full week before Phillis realized the full significance
of the courtroom episode." Why didn't you have more sense?"
she demanded, frustrated as she realized the incident was
barring him from every job he applied for.

She sympathized with him. How well she knew what it
was to have a mind not being used to capacity. Lately as she
tended Mary, she often wondered if the mentally well-en-
dowed weren't the unfortunate ones. Maybe, if one was not
continually thirsting for knowledge, was not born with intellectual curiosity, one could be more content performing
the menial tasks of everyday life.

But she was not. The compulsion to write was with her constantly, a relentless gnawing which plagued her as she went
about her daily tasks; but by the time she was ready to sit
down, she was too exhausted to think. Passages which had
flitted through her head all day were lost. Each morning she
promised herself she would stop and write them down, but
she had done nothing creative for more than a year now.

Jobs proved scarcer than either of them had ever imagined.
John made light of it at first, saying, "I've never had any
trouble finding work," but she panicked as he went out day
after day, returning with nothing other than an occasional
day's work at the docks, and their money dwindled.

"We've got to have something to live on," she told him.
"I've used the last of the money, and all it would buy was
three potatoes and a little corn."

"Then we'll eat corn and potatoes. At least it'll fill us up. I ate less than that many a time, and I lived through it."

"But my milk is drying up, and I know it's because I'm not eating enough. I can't wean Mary with summer coming on. She'll catch the flu sure." There was panic in Phillis' voice. At the bleak look in John's eyes, she would have given anything to take the words back. Far worse than the scarcity of food was his pride, which was shrinking daily.

In desperation, she went to see Reverend John. He was sympathetic but unable to promise her anything.

Reverend John's eyes were full of compassion. "I'm truly sorry, Phillis. If I can let you have some food to tide you over . . ."

"No, thank you. I know it's all you can do to feed your family with prices what they are. I'm sorry I bothered you."

"The Lord be with you," he said.

She refused all offers of help, knowing the idea of accepting it would crush John. She would find some way without living off charity. But it would have to be soon. If only she had written another book; for although she was attempting to write, the words simply would not come.

Surely, she thought, there must be someone who needs John, someplace where we can make a new start.

CHAPTER XXXVI

THE ANSWER CAME in July, an inconspicuous advertisement in the *Boston Gazette* for an able bodied man to help work a small farm in Wilmington, a village some fifty miles northwest of Boston.

Phillis was dubious when John told her he was interested in taking the offering.

"It will give us a chance to get back on our feet until I can get something better," he said when she voiced her doubts. "The owner is too old to manage without help. He offered to let me take whatever I need to feed my family." He strode restlessly back and forth in front of the fireplace. "At least it means a roof over our heads rent free."

Of course they must accept. They already owed two months back rent, and there was the matter she had not yet found the courage to mention. The morning queasiness in her stomach; the overwhelming sensation of sleepiness which plagued her in the afternoons were all the familiar signs of pregnancy. She prayed John would take it well. Perhaps this would solve the problem. There would be fresh air and enough to eat.

"The thing I havn't mentioned that means the most to me is I'll have time to study law at night, and make something of myself."

Now he looked like the John Peters she had fallen in love with, eyes alight, shoulders drawn proudly back. Others might call it arrogance. She called it a strong sense of pride. What right had she to hold him back? "Whither thou goest, I will go," she said, gaily. "Sssh, you'll wake Mary," she protested a moment later as he gathered her up in his arms and swung her around until she was breathless.

"I'll ignore her," he replied, carrying her over the bedroom threshold like a bride. "Tonight I share you with no one."

Later, as she reveled in the intimacy of being loved fully and completely, they made plans. It would be a new start for them.

She had not realized how many details needed attention moving far away. Each day was a hectic round of packing, farewells, decisions, leaving her scarcely a minute to herself.

"Phillis, we can't take all that," John said firmly when he saw her going through the contents of a trunk full of old manuscripts, books, and mementos.

"But I can't leave it behind," she wailed.

"Leave it with that relative of Susannah's who offered to let you store things. Remember?"

She felt as though she were leaving a bit of herself behind as the trunk was lifted from the cart and carried into Sarah's house the next day. "I do hope nothing happens to it," she said. "It's worthless to anyone else, but everything in it is a treasure to me."

"Don't worry, dear. It'll be safe here." Sarah paused as though trying to decide whether to say something, glanced at John, then lowered her head and spoke softly. "Phillis, dear, if things shouldn't work out in Wilmington, I hope you will keep in mind I'll always have room for you and the baby here. I know how much Aunt Susannah loved you, and I'd like to do what I can if I'm needed."

"Thank you, but I'm sure we won't need any help."

Wilmington, in the heart of Middlesex County, was a pretty place, its gleaming white church spires and the town meeting house visible long before they reached the village itself. A clean town with its neat rows of white clapboard houses set back behind prim picket fences over which ran riots of rambler roses, hollyhocks, and geraniums.

The Shelton place, a mile beyond, was a cluster of weather-beaten buildings surrounded by evenly furrowed fields, an apple orchard stretching out behind. Two stately trees shaded the house. Like a picture out of a book, Phillis thought as John pulled up in front of the lopsided gate and jumped to the ground. Phillis handed him Mary, then alighted herself.

The man who opened the door was bowed with age, his gait shuffling.

"We're the Peters, sir," John said.

"And I'm Isaac Shelton. Come in."

Phillis looked at him curiously as he admitted them to the dark olive green hallway and led them to the shabby sitting room. Shelton's sunburned face was pockmarked, and a sparse fringe of gray hair tickled his collar in back, but his faded blue eyes were still alert. Obviously, his mind had not slowed as quickly as his body.

"You have no idee how happy I am to see you folks." He glanced at Phillis and the baby. "This house has needed a woman ever since my wife was laid to rest three year ago." He offered them coffee. "I kinda got used to it with tea so scarce," he apologized as he poured it into chipped cups. Phillis took a sip and shuddered.

"Now I want you folks to know," Shelton said as he collected their cups, "I'll be out in the fields with you myself when I'm here. It's just I aint up to gettin' the whole crop in myself no more since my wife died and I like to visit my children now and then, but just between us, I can say there's none in the whole province with a better yield than mine." He motioned for them to follow as he showed them around the place.

Within a week, they felt settled. Mr. Shelton livened up mealtimes with his humorous stories gleaned from towns-people for generations back. He was delighted with Mary, holding her on his lap while he crooned to her and whittled toys to keep her amused while Phillis tended the house; and best of all, Phillis soon felt the beneath-the-surface panic she had lived with so long dissipating, replaced by a new serenity. Whether it was the clean fresh air or the fact that her parents were more relaxed, Mary settled down to a less demanding routine. Phillis and John once again found time to enjoy each other, their nights once more a time to express their love as joyously as they ever had.

Never had Phillis felt such ecstasy in being a woman as when they lay in bed together, the warmth of their love last-ing for hours afterward. By now she was sure the new baby was a certainty, and thankful John seemed happy about it.

"I guess so long as we've got one, she might as well have someone to play with," he had said when she told him.

CHAPTER XXXVII

THEIR FIRST WINTER on the farm proved to be
the coldest in Massachusetts history, but Phillis had never felt
more secure. The Shelton cellar was full to overflowing with
potatoes, squash, corn, the smokehouse with salted pork, hams,
and sides of beef, while the cupboards bulged with the fruits,
vegetables and preserves she had put up after a bumper crop.

But most exciting of all, she had sent her new manuscript
to White and Adams, overjoyed to find she had not lost her
flair with words. Almost as soon as they had settled at the
farm, she found herself able to write as freely as she once had
in the Wheatley household. The book was to contain not only
her poetry but copies of her correspondence with the countess, Mr. Occom, and other notables. "I hope they print it
soon," she said to John. "I can hardly wait to put it alongside
my first one."

George Washington Peters was born late in February.

How she wished that winter could have lasted forever; but
in less than a year it was almost as though their fortunes were
tied up with that of the Continental Army. Phillis knew it
was merely coincidence; still, it was the winter of 1780–81

when the army reached the low point of its existence. Although food and shelter were vastly improved over what was available the previous winter, they had suffered a series of demoralizing defeats.

Just before George's first birthday, Phillis received word from White and Adams they had been forced to abandon plans for publication of her book. There was simply not enough money in circulation to raise enough subscriptions to warrant printing it. Despite frantic efforts by her friends in Boston to secure the necessary amount, the project was simply not feasible. "Perhaps," the letter concluded, "if the financial picture improves, it will be possible to go ahead with it at a later date."

"What rotten luck," John stormed when she told him. "It was our chance to get out of this god-forsaken place."

"I thought you liked it here," she said, stunned.

"I've tried, Phillis. Honest to God I have, but I'm just not a farmer. All I see is bugs and weeds, and my back never stops aching. And I'm all thumbs. I couldn't even fix the fence the way he wanted yesterday." He didn't tell her how, as he stood listening to Shelton criticize it, he had suddenly blinked and could have sworn it was his pa standing over him yelling, "What are you good for? You can't even drive a nail in straight." He shrugged. "Oh, we'll stay here. What else can we do? But I don't like it."

It was like that day in London when a few words had shattered her beautiful world. Never in the months since their arrival had he voiced any dissatisfaction. Or was it because she was so preoccupied with her book, her pregnancy, and then the baby that she hadn't picked up the signals? She was angry with herself for mistaking her own contentment for a mutual one which had never existed.

She tried hard not to let John know how it affected her, but from that moment on she became acutely conscious of every little thing John and Shelton said to each other, calming John down when she sensed his quick temper rising.

But Shelton was pleased with the harvest. "Pretty good crop we got here," he had said, as they cut and stored the bales of hay. "Good thing too. At prices these days I can't afford to buy feed off'n anyone else."

"Be sure to check that barn roof, Peters," he said before he left to visit his daughter in New York. "A leak up there could ruin the hay and there'd be nothing left to feed the stock." He glanced up at the sky. "Better git to it today. Never know when a storm'll blow in this time of year."

John nodded. Shelton mounted his horse and rode off.

It was late afternoon when Phillis went out to feed the chickens. A sharp breeze rustled the leaves, and to the northeast a cloud moved briskly toward them.

Neither of them remembered Shelton's warning as they lingered over supper, enjoying the sound of the rain drumming on the roof.

Even when one of the cows sickened and died a week later, they didn't realize why. Only when Shelton returned, picked up a forkful of hay, sniffed and felt it, then turned to John, eyes blazing, did they know something was drastically wrong.

"This hay's wet," he roared. "Peters, I told you to check that barn roof. Didn't you do it? Hand me the ladder." Back on the barn floor he said grimly, "Wet hay rots. That's how the cow got sick. The whole lot is ruined. I'll have to buy more to feed the stock." His face was flaming with anger. "I reckon I should've hired me someone who knows something about farming." He glanced at Phillis then at Mary chattering at the chickens as she toddled among them. "Understand, Peters, if it weren't for your family I'd send you packing today, but I'll give you one more chance. Remember, though, one more time and I'll find me someone I can trust to do things right."

Phillis was close to tears as she felt her security topple like a castle built of sand.

She needed that security within these four walls, for she had realized for some time now the placid little town would never accept the Peters. Although she trudged to services at the small Congregational Church every Sunday, not a soul save the pastor and his wife spoke to her after services, and when she took her place in the pew assigned her at the rear of the church, those around her moved to create as much space between them as possible. Pastor Bradford finally told her the town had never seen free Negroes before, and were not Christian enough to accept them as brothers and sisters.

"They treat us like dirt," John said on the way home from one of their infrequent trips into town for supplies.

Fear stabbed at Phillis. "John, we've got each other. We make a good living off the farm. Let's try to be content with that."

"We're not likely to be on the farm much longer. Old Shelton doesn't think I'm much better than the dung I sweep up off the barn floor. He's just looking for an excuse to send us packing."

What was happening to them? They had seemed so safe and secure here. Why was it crumbling? Were they never to find where they really belonged? She was afraid to tell him the real reason for her fear — that she was once again with child.

News of the British surrender at Yorktown reached them in November. When the church bells started to ring, Phillis' first thought was fire, but there was no sign of smoke.

"The war is over," John told her when he came into the house a few minutes later. "The Peale boy just rode out from town with the news. Cornwallis surrendered to Washington more than two weeks ago."

"Thank God." Phillis said.

He shrugged. "What difference will it make? It won't change our lives any. Freedom is a word—nothing else."

CHAPTER XXXVIII

WINTER HAD PLUCKED the trees bare, the fields beneath the charcoal sky a barren expanse of brown broken only by an occasional dusting of snow like dabs of thin frosting in the hollows. Phillis added another log to the fire in a futile attempt to keep warm against the cold drafts blowing in around the windows and doors. She refilled the big copper kettle with water and set it on the hottest part of the fire. She always kept it handy in case little Eliza was seized with another of her frequent coughing spells.

"Did she have to be sickly like you?" John had yelled last night as Phillis walked the floor with her, terrified as the baby's lips had turned blue, her thin chest heaving with the effort it took to breathe during an attack.

Thank heaven she was all right now, her breathing normal, skin moist and cool. Born in June, nearly five weeks early, she had done well until the cold weather. If only she could survive long enough for warm weather.

"When we gonna eat, Mama?" Three-year-old George's brown eyes were enormous in his round face.

"In a few minutes," she answered, stirring the kettle of

soup, which was their mainstay these days. Last year's sparse crop meant they must make their small store in the cellar last until this year's could be harvested. She took down the last crock of apple butter. "How about some of this on your corn-bread tonight?" George's face lit up. It took so little to make him happy.

"Can I set the table now?" Mary asked.

Phillis' heart warmed at her small daughter's eagerness to help. Would John get home in time to eat with them, she wondered as she ladled the soup into bowls. He had gone into town for materials to fix the pasture fence, but that was hours ago. *Dear God, don't let him stop at McGillivary's again tonight,* she prayed.

But it would be a miracle if he didn't after this morning. Mr. Shelton was due back from New Haven any day, and John had promised to have the smokehouse whitewashed and the fence mended. He had done neither, and she had had to remind him again of the broken window in their bedroom. She had moved the cradle so the wind wouldn't blow directly on Eliza, but the room was so small it was impossible to avoid a draft.

"I'll do it," he had shouted when she had mentioned it again. "I told you I would when I got time."

"But you know how frail Eliza is." The thought of nursing her through another cold made her voice shriller than she had intended.

"Leave me be." He had grabbed his cloak and stalked out, slamming the door behind him.

Sleet had stung her face as she followed him out onto the porch and watched as he saddled and mounted the youngest of the horses. She watched him ride off, then whirled around and reentered the house, plunging into the closest task at hand in an attempt to submerge the disappointment and panic which was with her constantly these days.

At ten o'clock, the children asleep, she added another log

to the fire. If only she and John could talk about their problems; but whenever she tried he would shout, "I'm no simple-minded farm hand, and that's what even *you* think I am."

"That's not true," she would reply, but it was no use. It was as though her words triggered an emotional blackout. His eyes would go blank, as though shutters had been drawn over them.

John, she thought as she watched the flames burn higher, smoke being lured up the chimney, *you're a brilliant man, but you've got to come to terms with the world.* The clock chimed, the fire snapped, and outside she heard the wind begin to blow. Her heart was as cold as the weather as she made ready for bed. She looked down at Eliza. Should she take her into bed with her? No, it might disturb her sleep. She stuffed an old rag into the hole in the windowpane and put an extra quilt over Eliza before sliding into bed herself, aching for the warmth she and John should be sharing with each other.

It was not yet light when she awoke, sensing immediately she was still alone. She lay half awake for a moment, not comprehending the combination of sounds which had awakened her. Then the feeble cry, the bang of shutters against the house, and the staccato beat of rain against the windows penetrated. *Windows.* Her reaction was instantaneous as reality crashed through her consciousness. She was at the cradle in a second, shivering as she felt water on her bare feet and gusts of wind blowing in through the window.

She snatched Eliza up out of the wet bed and held her close. She wept as she felt shivers move up and down the tiny body long after Eliza slept.

By the next afternoon Eliza was burning up with fever, too weak to make more than faint kitten-like sounds as Phillis applied a damp cloth to the hot forehead. Already she could hear the first dread sounds of congestion as the husky cough forced up greenish mucus.

Mary and George watched as Eliza tried to nurse, but each time she grasped her mother's nipple, she was unable to breathe until she let go. Frustration turned the tiny face bright red.

There was still no sign of John. The rain had stopped, and Phillis could hear the cows bellowing. She sent Mary and George to feed the chickens, hoping Eliza would sleep long enough for her to feed the rest of the animals and milk the cows.

She heard Mr. Shelton return just before dark. Upstairs with Eliza, she was close to tears as she looked at the tiny, gaunt body.

"I'm up here," she called to Shelton.

"Mrs. Peters, what's wrong?" he cried. "Where's John?"

In halting words she told him of John's trip into town. "He must have been caught by the storm and decided to stay overnight."

Shelton muttered under his breath. Sensing she was near the breaking point, he quickly took charge.

"Mrs. Peters," he said later, "this child needs doctoring. I'd say your best bet is Boston. Is there someone there you can stay with?"

Phillis started to shake her head, then remembered Sarah's offer the day they had left. Eliza wheezed then, a tortured sound that tore through Phillis. "How soon can we leave?"

"Soon's we can git a few things together. You git the children ready and I'll hitch up the wagon."

She blessed his crisp air of authority. She was near the end of her strength, sheer necessity the only thing keeping her from total collapse.

Phillis gathered up enough clothing to last them a few days, then wrapped a piece of bread and some meat in a clean napkin and looked around for pen and paper.

Dear John, read the note she propped up against the sugar-bowl,

> I pray we reach a doctor in time for Eliza.
> Mr. Shelton is taking us to Boston. We'll
> stay with Sarah.

Within an hour they were in the creaking wagon, Eliza wrapped in several blankets, Phillis holding her beneath her cloak for warmth. George and Mary huddled against their mother on the high seat, a quilt thrown across their shoulders to keep out the cold.

The trip was sheer torture as Phillis tried to care for Eliza and quiet Mary and George's fears. What would John do when he found them gone, she wondered as they jolted over deep ruts, or perhaps he had never gone home. Perhaps he had been the one to flee Wilmington first. A year ago, leaving John would have been unthinkable, but, he was not the same man she had married, and if Eliza died, she could never forgive him for not fixing that window.

By the time they neared Boston, Phillis felt as though a massive weight was crushing her chest. Each agonized breath sent stabs of pain through her tortured lungs. Shelton drove as carefully as he could, but even so, the slightest jolt set her head afire with pain. She gritted her teeth, holding Eliza close as she struggled to draw in enough air. "I can't let go until we get there," she repeated over and over as she felt herself slipping into a gray mist.

She was only half aware of Sarah taking the baby from her when they reached the rambling old house on Bush Street. "You poor child," Phillis heard her say as she felt herself lifted by strong arms and carried into the house.

"Upstairs, the first room," Sarah directed. "I'll bring the children."

"Mr. Shelton?" Phillis whispered. "Could you . . . put him up tonight . . . he's been . . . so good . . ."

"Of course, dear. I'll take care of it. Now you're not to bother about a thing except getting some rest."

CHAPTER XXXIX

John let his horse gallop at top speed for a good quarter of a mile before slowing him down. He was tempted to turn back. He shouldn't have stormed out of the house like that, but damn it, he was sick of her nagging. Not that he didn't deserve it, but why couldn't she just yell at him. Then he could yell back, and they'd both get it out of their systems; but no, she'd just remind him in that sickening sweet way of hers that made him feel guilty because he'd neglected whatever it was she wanted him to do in the first place.

He had only meant to have one drink, two at the most at McGillivary's, but it was cold outside.

He was about to leave when McGillivary shoved a bowl of chowder and a loaf of still warm bread in front of him. "No use leaving on an empty stomach," he said. John attacked it with gusto, washing it down with more of the free flowing ale. Warmed by both fire and drink, he failed to realize until he started to leave that what had been merely a little sleet and a stiff breeze was now a real storm. John reached for the bottle and poured himself another drink, and then another. . . .

He recalled nothing of being put to bed, and on awakening

it took several minutes to realize the sun was high in the sky. He rolled over, but at the first movement it felt as though his head was being shot through a cannon, and he sank back on the pillow with a groan. By the time he cleaned up and got back the clothes McGillivary had washed for him, the afternoon was nearly gone.

The quiet unnerved him as he turned into the Shelton farm. Something was wrong.

"Phillis? George? Mary?" But even as he called, he knew he was alone in the house.

He almost didn't see the note. His hands shook as he unfolded and read it, then stared straight ahead. "But you know how frail Eliza is" hammering over and over at his mind. She'd warned him, and what had he done? Gone off and gotten drunk. What if Eliza died? Did that make him a murderer? Head in his hands, he sobbed like a small child.

He'd light out for Boston now. He was through with farming. After the mess he'd made of things, Shelton would be glad to get rid of him anyway. He'd have to go back to the grocery business. It was the only thing he'd ever done that he hadn't botched. The thought galled him, but if it meant he could have his family back, he'd swallow his pride and bow and scrape to any customer that came through the door.

More than once after his first week back in Boston, he'd walked past the house on Bush Street. Once he glimpsed the kids playing in the yard, another time, late at night, Phillis silhouetted against an upstairs window; but both times he fought the urge to go to them. Not until he was able to support them the way a man should.

For a month, it was days on the docks, or sweeping out a blacksmith shop. It made him wonder why he'd ever bothered to run away from the plantation. Only in a tavern, with a glass in his hand, did he begin to feel human again. He was about to sign on with a merchant ship when he heard about Cairns trying to sell his store on Fish Street, a rundown shabby little one-man operation. Buying it was out of the question. All he had was his last day's pay, and he'd been lucky at cards once or twice when the other guy was drunk enough, but if he could talk Cairns into holding off on the sale, let him work awhile . . . It was worth a try.

He blew the money on a new suit of clothes. He'd learned long ago looking successful was half the battle.

"What can you lose?" he asked when Cairns looked dubious. "You know what I did with my place on Queen Street. I can do the same for yours. Let me manage it, give me a year, and if I can't get the money together by then, you can sell it for twice what it's worth today."

His step was jaunty as he rounded the corner onto Pearl Street, tipping his hat to a buxom lady even though she crowded him off the sidewalk. After all, she might well end up as one of his customers.

On impulse, he turned into a small shop and selected a cake of sweet-smelling soap for Phillis, a ribbon for Mary's hair, a ball for George, then stopped. It was pretty sad when a man didn't know whether he still had three children or only two.

CHAPTER XL

IT HAD BEEN a full three days before Phillis awoke to sun streaming in, making dancing patterns on the highly polished floor. It took a few minutes to recall where she was as she looked at the robin's egg blue walls, the gleaming lowboy against the far wall, the china basin and pitcher on the washstand.

"You're awake. It's about time. How do you feel, dear?" The crinkles around Sarah's eyes deepened as she smiled.

"The children?" Phillis asked.

"Clamoring to see you. You gave me the fright of my life, Phillis Peters. Dr. Thornton's been in to see you everyday."

Doctor. "Eliza?" Phillis asked, bracing herself for the answer she dreaded.

"She's fine. Her fever's down, and she's taking nourishment."

Phillis lay back on the pillow, tears of relief in her eyes. The trip hadn't been in vain after all. "May I see the children now?" she asked.

Mary's kiss was dainty, as though she feared her mother would break in two. Not so George. He climbed up on the bed, knocking over a vase as he wiggled his way into her arms.

She hugged them both, a catch in her voice as she said, "It's so good to hold you again."

"Have you heard from John?" she asked Sarah later when they were alone.

"Nothing." Sarah's lips compressed into a thin line. "Phillis, it's none of my business, but I got the feeling Mr. Shelton was unhappy with him."

Phillis fingered the patchwork quilt as she told Sarah what had led to their flight. How good it felt to be able to talk to another woman. "I don't even know whether John ever got my note. The mood he was in when he left, he may not have gone back."

"Now you just put all that out of your mind for now," Sarah said crisply. "When you're stronger you can decide what you're going to do, but for now, concentrate on getting well."

"How can I ever repay you for your kindness," Phillis said. She watched Sarah refill the water pitcher, certain she could detect something of Susannah in her. She felt the tension drain out of her as she settled back against the pillows.

As her strength returned, she delighted in seeing Eliza seemed none the worse for her ordeal. She was even putting on weight. It must be the tonic Dr. Thornton had prescribed. Or maybe just a warm house and plenty of food. Whatever the reason, Phillis was thankful.

Mary and George adored Aunt Sarah, tagging along behind her every day to her schoolroom, where they sat in back, slates in front of them, as though they were pupils too. They seemed to accept Phillis' explanation that Daddy was still at the farm while they visited Aunt Sarah.

On New Year's Day, Phillis attended services at Old South, overjoyed to find that even after three years she was not entirely forgotten.

Later that week she was mending sheets when she heard the door clapper sound several times in rapid succession. Whoever it was must be terribly impatient or on extremely urgent business.

There was no warning, no premonition to prepare her. She merely opened the door, and there he was. Sober, nattily attired in his new coat and velvet breeches, his hair powdered and tied back in the latest style. On his face was the same charismatic smile that had first charmed her so long ago. Only his eyes hinted that he, too, had suffered.

He bowed slightly. "You're looking well, Phillis."

"So are you," she said when she could speak. She stepped aside. "Come in."

"Eliza?" he asked.

"She's going to be all right."

"Phillis, I'm sorry," he said as he stepped into the semi-dark hallway. "Can you ever forgive me?

"I don't know, John, I . . ."

"If I'd only realized . . ."

"It wasn't just the window," she said slowly.

He bowed his head slightly, an oddly subservient gesture for him, and she knew what coming here must have done to his pride. "I know. I should have been there when you needed me. It took your leaving to make me see that. Phillis, when I got back and found you and the kids gone . . . I nearly went out of my mind."

She leaned against the wall to steady herself.

"Phillis, don't you see my life is nothing without you to share it?"

They stood awkwardly in the small hallway facing each other, both aware of the charged atmosphere. "Come in here," she said, leading the way to the parlor. She purposely chose the wing backed chair by the fireplace, knowing if she sat on the sofa he would sit beside her. She needed space between them if she was to think clearly.

"Phillis, I know what you must think of me," he began.

"That doesn't matter."

"But it does. When I read that note, I knew I had to straighten myself out and come to you."

"It's been more than six weeks," she pointed out caustically.

"I had to find a job before I came." He paused. "I have one now."

Hope surged through her as he told of his arrangement with Cairns.

"But you didn't like the grocery business," she said.

"I guess I'm learning we can't always do what we want when there are others depending on us," he said slowly. "I know now I was a fool to let the other store go. I guess I've been ashamed of myself ever since, but I promise from now on it'll be different. I want to take care of you and the children."

She felt herself waver.

"It's Daddy." Mary had apparently heard his voice from upstairs. They heard her scramble down. He was on his feet as she burst through the door, eyes shining.

He caught her up in his arms and buried his face in her thick black curls. "God, how I've missed you."

Phillis' heart contracted painfully. How could she separate them? John's eyes were on her.

"Mama, can we go home again? All of us?" Mary pleaded.

Phillis raised her eyes to John's and nodded. "Just as soon as your Daddy finds us a house to live in."

She trembled as John's arms went around her and she raised her lips to his kiss, gentle, passionate, and protective, all at the same time.

CHAPTER XLI

1783

THE HOUSE JOHN FOUND for them on Brattle Street was small but adequate. Phillis at once set about adding the personal touches that made it a real home, delighted that John seemed content. Together they worked out a savings plan, the money earmarked toward the day John could buy the store.

"Cairns is nice enough, but he's an old doddard," he complained. "Won't put a cent into improvements. I can't wait until it's mine to do as I please." Night after night Phillis listened as he outlined his ambitious plans for expansion once he owned it. She rejoiced that their brief separation seemed to have brought them closer than ever; and while he still had a tendency to be somewhat overbearing and a trifle impatient with the children, she was content.

It was the end of July the following year when the dysentery epidemic struck. Before a week was out, the death bells tolled with scarcely a pause. John took ill first, and by the time he was back on his feet Eliza had it, then the other two.

For Phillis it was a nightmare of stifling hot nights when she never slept, tending first one, then another. Eliza's fever broke toward the end of the week, but neither Mary or George responded to treatment. They moaned as gripping pains ripped across their swollen bellies, their body discharges so copious Phillis was unable to keep them clean no matter how hard she tried. Even a sip of water brought a violent spewing of vital fluid from their gaunt dehydrated bodies.

George, his once chubby body skeletal, his yellowed skin stretched taut against his high cheekbones succumbed first. Surely he'll breathe again, Phillis thought frantically as she snatched him up in her arms, trying to breathe her own breath into him as she realized his chest no longer moved.

"It's no use," John said wearily, his face haggard in the flickering light of a stubby candle.

Only the knowledge Mary faced the same fate galvanized Phillis into action. "Get a doctor," she screamed. "Tell him our baby's dying." But even as he stumbled downstairs, she realized how futile it was. All the doctors in Boston were white, and not one of them was going to come tend a black baby when there were hundreds of white ones dying too. George's death wouldn't even be recorded in the registry. Only white people mattered. She sobbed. What kind of a God had put them in a world where the color of one's skin could deny them life?

Mary breathed her last as she lay in her mother's arms, her dark eyes glazed with pain.

He'd failed again. Heartsick, John took in the sight of Phillis still seated in the old pine rocker, their lifeless daughter cradled in her arms as she stared unseeing into the sultry night. Would she ever understand how hard he'd tried to get a doctor to come, even humbling himself to go to John Lathrop? But he, like every other doctor and clergyman, was out tending others.

For one agonizing moment, he thought Phillis was dead too. Frantic, he felt for a pulse. It was erratic, but there was one. Gently he took Mary from her. "Phillis?" he said, taking hold of her hand. In desperation, he poured out a jiggerful of brandy and forced it between her lips. "Phillis, wake up. I'm here."

The eyelids fluttered, but the eyes saw nothing. If only she would say something, anything. He needed her as never before, but she might as well have been stone. With a convulsive sob, he lifted her out of the chair and put her to bed.

It was John who arranged the services and accompanied the two bodies to the burying ground, while Phillis lay delirious with fever. Day and night, she tossed and turned on her bed. Even when the fever finally broke, she was aware of nothing except that she was enveloped in a swirl of fog, searching endlessly for her lost children, only occasionally aware of John bending over her, pleading with her to take some nourishment.

The day she aroused enough to see Eliza peering in at her, she realized God had mercifully spared one of their children, and that she still had a reason for living.

She was up and about again in a short time, but drained of the joy of living. She no longer thrilled to the sound of birds singing. She ate without tasting anything.

If only she and John could have shared their mutual grief, but she could not bring herself to talk about the children. As the days passed in monotonous succession, she realized an impenetrable wall had sprung up between them. One word, one touch from him might have enabled her to share, but he was as locked in as she. In the darkness of night, when they should have comforted each other, she lay awake, her heart crying out for what she had lost.

Even reading the scriptures failed to relieve the emptiness. She recalled a poem she had written years ago for a family who had lost a child.

> Where flies my James? 'Tis this I seem to hear
> The parents ask, "Some angel tell me where
> He wings his passage tho the yielding air?"

Methinks a cherub bending from the skies
Observes the question, and serene replies
"In heaven's high places your babe appears:
Prepare to meet him and dismiss your tears."
Shall not the intelligence your grief restrain
And turn the mournful to the cheerful strain?"

Had those words really offered any comfort to the be-
reaved? Or had they seen them as only the words of a naive
young girl who had never known the depths of real sorrow
and could not fully comprehend theirs?

As the first snow flurries deepened into a blanket of snow
and ice formed around the branches of trees, Eliza became the
focus of her mother's existence, her reason for living. Everything she thought, everything she did was for Eliza. If she
sneezed, Phillis jumped to fetch an extra shawl to wrap around
her.

"You're spoiling her," John accused one morning as they
finished breakfast. Phillis had been listening half-heartedly as
he outlined plans to secure a bank loan, but her attention was
on Eliza as she coaxed her to eat.

"I'm not spoiling her," she defended herself. "I'm just seeing she's properly taken care of. Maybe if I'd taken better
care of the others, they'd still be alive. Instead there's just
Eliza, and I won't risk losing her too."

"How about me? Phillis, I've been patient, but you're not
being fair. Life goes on, you know. Carrying on like this isn't
good for Eliza, and nothing can bring back the others."

She sighed as she rose to clear the table. "I'm sorry, John.
I'll try. I know you deserve more than I've offered lately. Tell
me about the store. Is Mr. Cairns still going to let you buy
him out?"

"That's what's been worrying me. He originally gave me
a year. Now he wants his money by the first of the month, or
he'll offer it to someone else."

"That's not fair," she cried. "Can we raise the money by then?" Since her illness she hadn't looked or even thought about the cache of money stashed behind the loose brick in their bedroom.

He nodded, but he had turned from her. His face was in the shadows, and she was unable to see his expression. Uneasiness jabbed her, but the moment to question slipped by. He was on his feet getting ready to leave.

She busied herself sorting clothes. She would ask him tomorrow. After all, wives weren't expected to know about their husband's business. Hadn't he told her that time after time?

The winter of 1783 was even colder than the one on the farm four years ago. A snowstorm no sooner blew itself out than another overtook it. Boston was like a white fairyland with sleighs the only feasible transportation. Their jingling bells added a festive note to even the darkest days.

In an effort to save money, John began looking for a cheaper place to live, for despite feeble attempts by the government to stem inflation, it took most of his pay to feed and house them.

They found a shabby flat on Centre Street near the waterfront, the entire building permeated with the overpowering odor of tar and brine mingled with fish and boiled cabbage. Phillis' heart sank as she looked at the cracked walls, peeling paint, and only one small fireplace for warmth.

As soon as they moved in she plunged into a frantic routine of scrubbing and polishing as though to make up in cleanliness what the rooms lacked in beauty.

John begged her to slow down and get more rest, for she was coughing again. At night she fell into bed exhausted, partly from hard work, partly from the realization that although they paid less rent, there was never enough money.

She sighed at the futility of it all. Was this what they had fought a war for? Less than three years since the cessation of hostilities, and the majority of people lived in poverty. Hardly a day went by that a business didn't fail, while old families were forced to take in roomers just to get money for food. She couldn't help contrasting this to life before the war.

Later, when the fire was only ashes, she decided to write to Nat. She had heard nothing from him since shortly after Mary's death, but surely if he knew of their plight he would help. Forcing back her pride, she told him what had led to their present predicament.

"I am not asking for a gift," she wrote, "only a loan to tide us over until John can buy the store."

After inquiring about Sally's health and their mutual London friends, she closed with, "Your loving sister and humble servant."

Winter dragged on. Heavy snowdrifts made most roads impassable. Even when they were cleared, sheets of ice made them unsafe for anything but emergency travel. With almost no way to bring it in, firewood became scarce, supplies so short a wagonload would come in and be sold before most people even knew about it. To conserve heat, Phillis wrapped a piece of flannel around her chest and kept the fire as low as she dared. It reminded her of the year she and Master John had sat out the siege on King Street.

She was worried about John. Never had she seen him like this. He was either so depressed he scarcely knew she was there, or so on edge he was impossible to live with.

Remembering the chill which had nearly cost Eliza's life, Phillis became obsessed with keeping the child warm. She put a layer of oiled paper over every window, and made new quilts out of old patched clothes gathered from church families. Patiently, night after night, she sat by the fire sewing endless squares together, each night's work representing a bit more warmth to keep their one remaining child safe from the cold.

By the middle of March, it was clear John's behavior was not going to change. She felt a cold fringe of fear around her heart as he left early in the morning, returning home long after dark. They scarcely spoke, and his veiled eyes gave no clue to what his thoughts were.

She said nothing until the day he turned on Eliza. It happened so fast Phillis was stunned as a stream of milk from Eliza's overturned cup cascaded across the table to where John sat reading the paper. Before Phillis could stop him, he sprang up and cuffed Eliza so hard she reeled back, knocking over a chair.

"Clumsy oaf," he shouted.

"Leave her alone," Phillis cried. "She couldn't help it."

"Look what she's done to my only decent breeches."

"What's more important? Your clothes or your daughter?" Eliza's lips quivered, and a tear slid down one cheek. Phillis picked her up, but she wiggled down, grabbed a rag, and began wiping up the puddle on the floor, hiccoughing as she watched her father dab at the spreading stain with a towel.

Phillis helped her clean up, then took her into the other room out of John's way.

If only she would hear from Nat.

CHAPTER XLII

SHIFTLESS ... DRIFTER ... Phillis cringed as she
heard the whispered words, painfully aware of the awkward
silence the moment she appeared at the marketplace, the
church foyer, and wherever else people were gathered. With
great effort at pretending dignity, she drew herself up and
ignored them.

Like everyone else, she had just begun to hope the long
winter was over when another storm struck, this one the
worst yet. The wind howled for three days, and whole portions of the city were isolated, the heavy snow making it impossible to see more than a few feet.

Phillis was frantic. Despite the way she had hoarded it, their
scanty supply of wood was nearly gone. And as if this were
not enough, John had not gone to work for three days. He
told her his stomach was bothering him.

Just before noon there was a tap at the door. Opening it
she was astonished to see her old church friends, Lydia and
Ezra Price.

"Phillis, dear, how are you?" Lydia kissed her. "Ezra and
I were down this way and thought we'd stop by." She shifted

the covered basket she carried to the other arm.

"How nice. Do come in." Phillis stepped aside, embarrassed at being seen in such a shabby dress. She saw their quick glance around the drab room, the attempt to conceal their dismay.

"Will you have a cup of tea?"

"No, thank you. We can't stay. We were just outside town and brought back a load of wood . . . ."

Seeing Phillis start to shake her head, Lydia's tone became more emphatic. "Now we won't take 'no' for an answer. Fact is, Ezra bought so much we've no place to keep it. He thought you might take it off our hands." She handed Phillis the basket. "And as long as I was baking this morning, I thought I'd bring you folks some." She laughed nervously. "With all our children grown and gone, we just don't need anywhere near what we used to."

Phillis knew it was nothing of the sort. Extra wood? Not this winter.

"I left the wood out in the shed there beside the building." Ezra said. "It has to be split, but that's no problem. I 'spect Mr. Peters can do it."

"Thank you," Phillis said.

"No trouble at all," Ezra said. "Like Lydia says, we got more'n we need ourselves. Glad to share it."

John emerged from the bedroom just as they rose to leave.

"John, you remember the Prices," Phillis said.

His nod was curt.

"They've brought us some firewood."

"Firewood?" John asked. "What for?"

"Well, fact is, we heard you might be able to use it," Ezra began.

John turned on Phillis. "What have you been doing?" he demanded. "Prattling to every gossip in town?"

Anger exploded in Phillis like the eruption of lava. "That's enough, John." Her voice was scissor sharp. Turning to their guests, she said, "You must excuse him. He's not feeling well."

"That's quite all right. We understand." Lydia's face was pasty white, her glance one of contempt for John, pity for Phillis. "Come, Ezra, we must be going."

"What's the matter with you? How dare you shame me in front of my friends like that?" Phillis cried as the door closed behind the Prices. How she hated her own weakness. If she'd had a grain of sense she'd have stayed with Sarah.

John's chin was thrust out belligerently. "What right had they to assume I'm a charity case? Don't they think I can support my family? Well, I can. Without any help from them. You have something to eat, don't you? A place to sleep."

"Just barely. And for how long? You won't even go to work."

She knew by his eyes she had hit her mark, but she made no move to soften her words.

Two nerve wracking months later, she answered an early morning knock at the door.

"This where John Peters lives?" asked the taller of the two men standing there.

"He's still asleep. What do you want?"

"We've come to arrest him."

"Arrest him? What for?"

"For not paying his debts. Says here he owes over a hundred pounds."

"It's a mistake. We haven't much, but we owe no one," she cried.

"There's no mistake, Phillis." John's voice behind her was muffled. She listened, horrified, as he explained what had been keeping him out all hours. "After the bank turned me down, I knew I had to get the money some other way. I was lucky at first. Won almost enough, but then last week . . ." his voice broke . . . "I just meant to play one more hand, honest . . ."

Nausea rose in her throat. "Why didn't you tell me?" she asked, struggling to control her emotions.

She was mortified at having the two men from the Governor's office witness this intimate scene. They had remained by the door, hats in hand. Now the tallest one stepped forward. "Sorry, M'am. Peters, you'll have to come with us."

Fear gripped Phillis as the trio went out into the street. She had heard stories of how they threw men into debtors' prison, sometimes keeping them there for years. There was only the little money he had earned this past week. After that was gone . . .

"Do you have the means with which to pay these debts?" the judge asked.

"Phillis had to strain to hear him mumble, "No, your honor."

"John Peters, I sentence you to an indeterminate time in debtors' prison."

He looked at her wordlessly, shock, despair, and anger all mirrored simultaneously for one single instant, then his eyes went blank; and in one final show of arrogance he threw back his head and glared at the guards as he was led away.

Phillis was scarcely aware of anything except that there had been no endearment, no farewell from him as he went through the door.

CHAPTER XLIII

PHILLIS LOOKED AT HER REFLECTION in the cracked mirror and sighed. Few would believe she was just past thirty. Her once lustrous hair was now dull and shot through with gray; and a spidery web of criss-cross lines radiated from the corner of each eye. In the dark eyes which gazed back she could see nothing of the girl who had once danced in the royal manors of England, and been feted in the drawing rooms of Boston society.

A painful coughing spasm brought tears to her eyes as she pulled her bodice tighter across her nearly non-existent bosom to hide the bones below the hollow in her throat.

In her hand she clutched the letter from London, the one on which she had pinned her hopes of paying off John's debts so he could be free.

> "It pains me to tell you," Sally had written, "that my dear husband, Nathaniel, passed away three months ago of consumption. Please forgive my not writing until now, but his death was such a shock I have been indisposed.
> I am deeply grieved to hear of your sad plight and regret I am not in a position to offer assistance, but you

must understand that our fortunes were adversely affected by the war; consequently, I find myself in a position not unlike your own, and were it not for the generosity of my father, I should have barely enough to live on myself..."

Dear Nat. The last of the Wheatleys, the one who had given up his country for his beliefs. Now he was gone too. Nothing remained of the warm wonderful family she had been part of for so long. John and Eliza were all she had left.

Or did she have John? An indeterminate sentence meant there was no assurance when he would be given his freedom—if ever, for it was common knowledge that persons jailed for indebtedness could rot there for years, apparently forgotten, as judges concerned themselves with more pressing matters.

With her last hope of help from Nat gone, she turned to the problem of earning a living for herself and Eliza. The last of their money was gone; in fact, she was staying there only because of the generosity of the landlord.

Money. Their food was running out. Their cupboards would be bare now if the church hadn't sent a basket of staples last week. Even with that, Eliza was always hungry, and Phillis had grown used to the stomach cramps she suffered from her diet of tea and a little bread.

"Surely, Phillis, there must be someone you could call on for help," the church sexton had said when he delivered the basket.

Phillis had shaken her head.

"Forgive me for suggesting this, but I understand you lived with the Lathrop family before your marriage. He is a Christian man, and surely if he realized...".

"No, please. You mustn't say anything to Mr. Lathrop. I've heard he's remarried and fallen on rather hard times himself with eight children to feed."

"But when you were with his wife's family for so many years..."

"Mr. Hunt, I have no doubt he would help, or at least try to," she had said, "for he's one of the kindest men I've ever known; but it would be taking food out of the mouths of his own family, and I . . ." "I couldn't do that."

"I understand. There's no one else?"

She thought of the people she might have squelched her pride and called on a few years ago, but Sarah had remarried and moved to Quincy with her new husband and stepchildren. Ezra Price was dead, and Lydia had gone to live with one of her boys.

She shook her head. "There's no one." She managed a weak smile. "Don't worry. We'll be all right." She said it with more conviction than she felt. "The Lord will watch over us."

She would seek work as a governess or tutor. With her experience there must be some place for her, but she soon found that most of the old families were living in genteel poverty. Few could afford to hire anyone, and those who could, preferred young gentlemen of their own race, usually students from Harvard. Everywhere she went, she met with polite but firm refusal.

At last she resorted to looking for day work. She had been thoroughly trained in caring for a home. It would earn her enough money to keep the two of them alive. But to her dismay, even this kind of work was far from easy to find.

She was desperate the morning she trudged up the narrow street on the back side of Beacon Hill. Through the church, she had heard of a woman who had opened a new boarding house and needed someone to clean and launder.

"You sure you're strong enough?" Mrs. McGuire's piercing black eyes scrutinized Phillis' spare frame. Phillis sat rigid, knowing one cough during the interview could cost her the job.

"Oh, yes, M'am. I may not look strong, but I am. I kept up the whole house for my master before he died. The Wheatley house on King Street." She said it tentatively, wondering if

the name meant anything, but apparently Mrs. McGuire was
one of the many who had poured into Boston after the war,
for she shook her head, her sharp features showing no recognition of the name so familiar to old time Bostonians.

"Well, I suppose I can give you a try," she said, "but if
you can't do the work, you'll have to go. I can't coddle
anyone."

"Yes'm, I understand." Phillis looked down quickly, trying
to summon courage to tackle the hardest part of the interview.
"There's just one thing," she began, her insides shaking. "I
have a little girl four years old. I wonder, would it be possible
for me to bring her with me during the day? I have no one
to leave her with, and I ..." her voice faltered. So much
depended on the answer.

"Impossible," snapped Mrs. McGuire. "How can you work
with a child tagging after you?" She shook her head. "No,
I've seen mothers try that. They end up spending most of
their time wiping noses and running after their children."

Phillis was desperate. She *had* to have this job.

"Mrs. McGuire, I promise I can work just as well with
Eliza along. She's quiet, and she'll even help dust—she's real
good at that." Panic kept her talking to stave off the answer
she feared. "She can fetch things and polish just as well as
any older girl. Please, Mrs. McGuire. I promise she'll be no
bother."

The woman's face softened a trifle. "You can bring her,
and we'll see how it works out," she said finally, "but if she
slows you down ..." her tone left no doubt she considered
the experiment a dubious one.

Once on the job, fatigue dominated Phillis' every waking
hour, for the work was hard; and at the end of the day, she
still faced the long tiring walk home. By the time they reached
there, Eliza would be whimpering with weariness, and Phillis
was too tired to even fix a bite to eat before falling into bed.

But it was worth it at the end of the month when she received her first salary. It was not much, but adequate for their needs. There was a spring to her step as she and Eliza strolled through the quiet streets planning what to buy.

Near the end of August, she found a small furnished room closer to work, so the walk home became a more pleasant one.

"Is Daddy coming soon?" Eliza renewed her persistent question and searched her mother's face for reassurance.

"I hope so," Phillis answered. "I hope so."

CHAPTER XLIV

1785

"WAKE UP, MAMA. It's time to go to work."

Phillis groaned and pulled the thin quilt up over her head.

"Mama, it's daylight."

Wearily, Phillis swung her legs over the edge of the bed. Her heart warmed as she watched Eliza, on tiptoe, pour her wash water into the chipped basin.

"Thank you." Phillis forced herself to put one foot in front of the other. She coughed violently, using a handkerchief to catch the forced up plug of mucus.

Fortified with a cup of tea, they went downstairs to begin their walk through the early morning quiet. The streets were nearly deserted, except for an occasional watchman or young boy on his way to sweep chimneys. Mice scurried at sound of their footsteps, stray cats rummaged through garbage dumped in the back alleys, and birds twittered in the crisp chill air.

Phillis pulled the ragged woolen shawl closer around her

shoulders. She hoped it was not to be another winter like last year.

Her hours were seven in the morning until seven at night; but it was often nine or more before they finally started home, her muscles crying out for rest, her back bent with fatigue. She had not heard from John for more than a year now, since he had been transferred to the prison on Castle Island for his participation in an escape plan discovered by one of the guards. Since then her letters to him had been returned unopened. She had sought information, but beyond being assured he was alive and in reasonably good health, she could learn nothing.

Mrs. McGuire waylaid Phillis as soon as she arrived. "Mr. Stevens is complaining his linen wasn't changed yesterday, Phillis. Be sure you do it first thing today. Oh, and don't forget to polish the furniture in the downstairs parlor." She fired the orders in rapid succession, then shook her head. "I don't know what's happened to you lately, Phillis. You used to do such a fine job, but lately you're neglecting things. You know I pride myself on a clean place. Cleanliness is next to godliness, my mother always said."

Phillis grew thinner, her clothes hanging on her by the time the first snow flurries fell. Now there was another worry— keeping enough wood for the fire. She hired a boy to bring up the first load. She could continue to do that so long as her money held out, but she shivered as she recalled the struggle they had gone through to keep warm on Centre Street. She worried constantly about Eliza catching cold. She was still small for her age and on the frail side. If Eliza got sick, how could she take care of her and still work? The thought tormented her as the thermometer dipped lower, and ice formed on the rivers.

By early November, she found herself so weary, just taking another step or lifting a broom became a formidable task. She had always kept their room neat, but now she let it go, not even bothering to pull up the bedcovers in the morning, for it took precious energy she must save for her job.

"Let me do that, Mama." Eliza waited on her hand and foot when they were home. Despair flooded her. Just taking care of Eliza was more than she could manage these days.

A storm struck during the night, and by morning everything was blanketed under thick wet snow. Phillis dressed Eliza as warmly as she could, wrapped her shawl around her shoulders, and fortified herself with an extra cup of tea.

Phillis ducked her head against the wind as they plodded uphill in the ankle deep snow. Her flimsy shoes and skirt were soaked. She had brought a change of clothes for Eliza, but all she could hope for was to shed her shoes once she got there.

She sat Eliza by the kitchen fire as soon as they arrived, but she had time only to warm her hands before scurrying off to the laundry room. By the time she slipped back to the kitchen for her noon meal, she was thoroughly chilled, her feet and legs so cold there was no feeling left in them.

She worked as fast as she could, conscious only that she must keep up or lose her job. She couldn't let that happen.

Three days later, she was unable to rise out of bed. She lifted her head off the pillow, but it made her so dizzy she sank back moaning. She must get to work somehow. She could tell by Eliza's breathing she had taken cold. She felt her forehead and thanked God it felt cool to the touch.

She finally managed to sit up on the side of her bed, then doubled over as a fit of coughing drained her strength. Through sheer will power she managed to dress herself, then wake Eliza. If only she didn't have to take her out in this weather; but she had no choice.

The walk to work was agonizing. Carrying Eliza so she wouldn't get wet, she had to stop many times to rest. The cook gaped at them as they came through the door.

"Phillis, you aint in no shape to work today."

"I must," she answered, fighting the dizziness which threatened to make her lose her balance whenever she moved too quickly.

"Then at least have a cup of tea and a piece of this salt bread before you begin." Seeing Phillis glance toward the door, she added, "Now don't you worry about herself. She's upstairs, and she'll never know."

Phillis sat down gratefully. The hot tea warmed her, giving her at least the illusion of a little strength. Knowing how Mrs. McGuire detested children with runny noses, she said, "Keep Eliza here in the kitchen where it's warm, will you?"

" 'Course I will, deerie. Don't you worry about a thing."

Birdie put more water on to boil. "Better be careful of herself today, though. She must've had a run in with one of the boarders. She's sure enough got the devil in her, she has."

Thanking her for the warning, Phillis hurried upstairs where Mrs. McGuire found her. Phillis coughed, a great hacking spasm that set her whole body shaking and left her weak and dizzy. The room danced in front of her eyes. She caught hold of the chest beside her, swaying it just enough to send one of Mrs. McGuire's prized salt glazed figurines crashing to the floor.

"Oh, no..." Mrs. McGuire's anguish was genuine.

Phillis stared in horror at the fragments scattered across the floor. "I'm sorry, I..."

"What is wrong with you, Phillis?" A white ring encircled Mrs. McGuire's compressed lips. "You can't keep up with the work, you break things." She bent down and picked up the largest piece of the shattered ornament. "This belonged to my mother," she said in a hushed voice. "She gave it to me the day I left County Cork." Her voice hardened. "You know, of course, that I have been dissatisfied with your work for some time now."

Knowing what was coming, Phillis stood mute, stunned by the rapidity with which it had happened.

Mrs. McGuire straightened up, still holding the broken fragments. "You're in no condition to work anymore today. If you'll come with me, I'll pay you through yesterday, and you can go on home."

Phillis followed her downstairs, certain her legs would give out from under her. To Eliza she merely said, "Come, dear, we're going home."

She was thankful it was downhill most of the way as they slowly sloshed through the snow, pausing every few minutes to rest. As they started up the rickety flight of steps to their room, she had the ridiculous feeling they stretched every bit as high as the Gates of St. Peter.

"Hurry up, Mama." Eliza was already half way up. Phillis still stood on the bottom step fighting for breath. Her chest heaved, and her lungs felt as though they would burst as she began her laborious ascent, clutching at the rail for support.

She had no idea how long she lay in bed. Her days had become an endless succession of pain and futility, like beads strung one after another. She was conscious only that Eliza, her emaciated body aflame with fever, lay huddled next to her, an occasional whimper the only sound from her for hours at a time.

Phillis licked her cracked lips and raised her head off the pillow, then sank back exhausted as another coughing spell made her struggle to breathe.

Opening her eyes, she tried to focus on the other side of the room. The fireplace was dark. She had burned the last of the wood yesterday—or was it the day before? Her glance moved over the washstand, her toilet articles strewn carelessly over it, then to the corner where dirty clothes still lay in a disheveled heap, for she had been too weary to pick them up. By the fireplace a pitcher and one battered pan, two cracked mugs, two spoons, and two chipped bowls constituted their kitchen ware. The cupboard doors hung open exposing the bare shelves.

Her glance swept to the dresser, one carved leg broken off. She had propped it up with a brick, but it still sat lopsided against the wall. On top were her beloved books, their worn but luxurious bindings a strange contrast to the rest of the furnishings. Even with eyesight dimmed by fever, she could make out the titles. Her own book, *Poems on Various Subjects, Religious* and *Moral;* next to it, *Don Quixote* and *Paradise Lost,* and the Wheatley bible. Every title brought back happy memories. She relived in her mind the day Mr. Bell had given her the first copy of her book. She heard again the Countess' words, "This is just the beginning for you, Phillis . . ." She stood with John again as they recited their marriage vows, played once more with Mary and George in the spacious meadow in Wilmington, picking apples off the trees and giggling as they bit into them.

Eliza gave a faint mewing cry, shivered, and nestled closer to her mother. Phillis pulled the ragged quilt higher, then dozed off again.

It was dark when she awakened. The cold was so intense she could see white rings form when she breathed. An icicle cracked as it broke off the big oak tree just outside the window. A single shaft of moonlight made a narrow path across the floor, illuminating the single candlestick on the dresser.

She reached for Eliza. The child lay perfectly still, strangely cool to the touch. Alarm prickled Phillis' scalp. "Eliza," she whispered hoarsely. "Eliza, . . ." She searched frantically for a pulse. There was none. "Dear God . . . her anguished scream echoed in her ears . . . "my baby . . ."

Frost glittered on the windowpanes. She wondered why the tears did not come. She had lived thirty one years and for what?

Not to bear children, for none were left to carry on. What then? Every sense in her suddenly heightened. For a split second she seemed to see Miss Susannah, Master John, Sukey, Dora, Mary, Nat, all smiling at her from a great distance.

What were they trying to tell her? She blinked, for the illusion was gone as quickly as it had come.

With one last effort, she opened her eyes and looked at the volume of poetry on the dresser. Was that what God had intended for her to do? Use the talent He had given her? Spread the beauty of words, the love of God. Maybe her life hadn't been wasted after all. Although she had no children to leave behind, she had left her words, her thoughts, her gift to posterity in the form of poetry. She had shown the world that intellectual ability and achievement are not confined to any one race of people.

She touched the still figure beside her and grasped the stiffening fingers. Eliza was where she would never be cold or hungry again. Phillis closed her eyes finally as a beautiful sensation of peace and warmth crept over her.

THE END

EPILOGUE

On the Thursday after Phillis Wheatley's death, a notice appeared in the Independent Chronicle:

> Last Lord's Day, died Mrs. Phillis Peters (formerly Phillis Wheatley), aged thirty-one, known to the world by her celebrated miscellaneous poems. Her funeral is to be this afternoon, at four o'clock, from the house lately improved by Mr. Todd, nearly opposite Dr. Bullfinch's at West Boston, where her friends and acquaintances are desired to attend.

Phillis Wheatley was carried to her last earthly resting place, without one of her friends of her prosperity to follow her, and without a stone to mark her grave. Her child was buried beside her.

In the December 1784 issue of the Boston Magazine a poem appeared in its pages. It was entitled *"Elegy on the Death of a Late Celebrated Poetess"* and it was simply signed "Horatio." Some of the lines read:

> . . . . PHILLIS tun'd her sweet mellifluous lyre;
> (Harmonious numbers bid the soul aspire)
> While AFRIC'S untaught race with transport heard,
> They lov'd the poet, and the muse rever'd.
>   What tho' her outward form did ne'er disclose
> The lilly's white, or blushes of the rose;
> Shall sensibility regard the skin,
> If all be calm, serene, and pure within? . . .
> Free'd from a world of wo, and the scene of cares,
> A lyre of gold she tunes. a crown of glory wears.
>   Seated with angels in that blissful place,
> Where she now joins in her Creator's praise. . . .

BIBLIOGRAPHY

Renfro, *Life and Works of Phillis Wheatley*, Books for Libraries Press, N.Y. 1969

Phillis Wheatley Poems and Letters, First Collectors Edition, Edited by Chas. Fred Heartman with Appreciation by Arthur Schomberg

Light, *Memoirs and Poems of Phillis Wheatley*, Memoirs by Margaretta M. Odell, Boston, 1834

The Poems of Phillis Wheatley, Introduction by Julian D. Mason, Jr., Univ. of No. Carolina Press, Chapel Hill, N.C., 1966

Poems Religious and Moral by Phillis Wheatley with Memoirs by W. A. Jackson, W. H. Lawrence & Son, Denver, 1897

Boggins, *The Negro Author*, Columbia University Press, N.Y., 1931

Rollins, *Famous American Negro Poets*, Dodd Mead & Co., N.Y. 1965

References used to recreate colonial life in Boston:

Seaberg, *Boston Observed*, Beacon Press, Boston, 1971

Bearse, *Massachusetts A Guide to the Pilgrim State*, Houghton-Mifflin, Boston, 1971

Earle, *Home Life in Colonial Days*, The MacMillan Co., N.Y., 1898

Tunis, *Colonial Living*, World Publishing Co., N.Y., 1957

Speare, *Life in Colonial America*, Random House, N.Y., 1963

Robbins, *History of Second Church*, John Wiles & Son, Boston, 1852

Old South Church Catalog, Boston, Rockwell & Churchill, City Printers

Boston—Births from AD 1700 to AD 1800, Rockwell & Churchill, City Printers

Boston—Marriages from AD 1700 to AD 1809, Vol. 28-30, Rockwell & Churchill, City Printers

Foote, *Annals of Kings Chapel*, Vol. II, Little Brown & Co., Boston, 1896

Dictionary of American Biography, Vol. V, VI, VII, Chas. Scribners Sons, N.Y. 1933-34

The Annals of America, Vol. II, Resistance and Revolution, Encyclopedia Brittanica, 1968

Forbes, *Paul Revere & the World He Lived In*, Houghton-Mifflin, Boston, 1942

Pearson, *Everyday Life in Colonial America*, G. P. Putnams Sons, N.Y., 1965

Alderman, *Samuel Adams, Son of Liberty*, Holt Rinehart & Winston, 1961

Wagner, *Patriots Choice, The Story of John Hancock*, Dodd Mead & Co., N.Y., 1964

Encyclopedia o fAmerica, Facts & Dates, Thos Y. Crowell, 1958

Bergman, *Chronological History of the Negro in America*, Harper & Row, N.Y., 1969

Books used for the background of the Revolution:

Blivens, *The American Revolution, 1760-1783*, Random House, N.Y., 1958

Russell, *Lexington, Concord, & Bunker Hill*, Harper & Row, N.Y., 1963

Fleming, *Now We Are Enemies*, St. Martin's Press, N.Y., 1960

Miller, *Origins of the American Revolution*, Little, Brown & Co., Boston, 1943

Bowen, *John Adams & the American Revolution*, Little Brown & Co., Boston, 1950

Pearson, *Those Damned Rebels*, G. P. Putnams Sons, N.Y., 1972

Flexner, *George Washington in the American Revolution*, Little, Brown & Co., Boston, 1967

Griswold, *The Night the Revolution Began*, S. Greene, Brattleboro, Vt., 1972

Chidsey, *Seige of Boston*, Crown Publishers, N.Y., 1966

Hansen, *The Boston Massacre*, Hastings House, N.Y., 1970

Peckham, *The War for Independence*, University of Chicago Press, 1958

Sources used for the portion set in London:

Burton, *The Pageant of Georgian England*, Chas. Scribners Sons, N.Y., 1967

Leckey, *Life & Times of Selina, Countess of Huntingdon*, 1839-40, History of England—18th Century, Vol. III

White, *Horizon Concise History of England*, American Heritage Pub., subs. McGraw-Hill, N.Y., 1971

McConnell, *John Wesley*, Abingdon Press, N.Y., 1939

Stevens, *The History of the 18th Century Movement Called Methodism*, History of Methodism, Carleton & Porter, N.Y., Vol. I 1858, Vol. II 1859

Dictionary of National Biography, Vol. V, VI, XXI, Oxford University Press, 1917

Valentine, *Lord North*, University of Oklahoma Press, 1969

Van Dorn, *Benjamin Franklin*, Viking, N.Y., 1938